ASK CURTIS

🐾 🐾 🐾

By Curtis the Dog

With an assist from his human
Dan Gersten

Dogwalk Press
Agoura Hills, CA 91301

Ask Curtis

Dogwalk Press
an imprint of Dan Gersten & Associates, LLC

For information address:
Dan Gersten & Associates, LLC
29636 Quail Run Drive
Agoura Hills, CA 91301
www.askcurtisthedog.com

ISBN:0-9766846-0-8

Printed in the United States of America

Dear Curtis,

Heard some scuttlebark that you were writing "Ask Curtis," a book for dogs and other animals (including humans). Just want to let you know that those of us who meet in the local dog park each day are behind you and hope the humans who read your book can appreciate the need for some canine wisdom in this man-eat-man world. Best of luck.

Jake and His Dog Park Buddies

Dear Jake and Buds,

Thank you! Also hoping that those who read this book have, themselves, some good old fashioned common dog-sense and can sniff out the value in dispensing important information in a novel, fun and entertaining way. Also hope they like dogs!

Curtis the Dog

"Outside of a dog, a book is probably man's best friend, and inside of a dog, it's too dark to read."
- Groucho Marx

A great big slobber kiss to Frisco who paved the way for my human to understand me and enable me to bark my dog-sense.

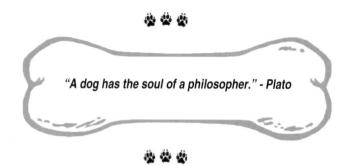

"A dog has the soul of a philosopher." - Plato

Lots of licks for Beth Spector, Randy VyDuna, Ashley Rogers, Karen O'Malley, Matt Gersten & David Chubb, DVM.   Special treats to the following for their support and encouragement: Heather Gersten Perry, Renee Selan, Liz Stern, Richard Brooks, Geri Bonenfant, Sally Cabrera, Laura Petrucci, Lori Simon, Harold "Hesch" Steinberg, Les & Fern Getto, Joan & Peter Beckerman, Matt Mack, Cheryl Calabrese and Mitch Schwartz.

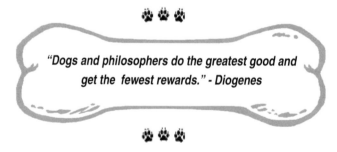

"Dogs and philosophers do the greatest good and get the fewest rewards." - Diogenes

The information presented in this book has been collected and compiled from publicly available sources and, where appropriate, has been reviewed and approved by a veterinarian, trainer or other pet care professional.

INTRODUCTION/ABOUT THE AUTHOR

Woof!

I'm Curtis and it's believed that I'm a seven-to-nine year old Collie-Golden mix, though only the great dog god Canus knows my age and what else I may have in my DNA!

I was "rescued" from a local animal shelter about 6-1/2 years ago after having been found "on the street," running free and without any identification. And, I must say that when I first moved to my new home and met my new humans, a married couple with a 10-year old son, I wasn't in a good state of mind or on my best behavior.

I didn't wag my tail. I cowered when anyone made a gesture toward me, even if it was to scratch my ear or rub my head. I didn't come to the dinner table when they were eating and I wouldn't take any treats or people food that were offered. Worse still, whenever I was left alone in the house, I inevitably destroyed something: a lamp, a leather address book, window blinds and screens, etc. And, on walks, I would growl and make menacing moves toward other dogs even though they just wanted to say "woof" to a potentially new friend in their neighborhood.

Then, something awful happened that caused me to be reflective and introspective, express my feelings, take stock of my life and recognize my calling to help others, especially my fellow canines.

My female human, who some would call my "mom," became ill about five months after having rescued me and passed away ten-months later, a relatively small time in the life of a human but about four-to-six years or so of a dog's life. The bottom line was that I hardly got to know her.

During her illness, there were always people in the house, which enabled the social animal in me to emerge. But, more importantly, her illness taught me to appreciate my life, both the good and the bad, and not to dwell on what could have happened to me as a pupster when I may have been abused and abandoned.

Rather, I learned that life, whether it be a dog's or human's, is precious and that we never really know how long it will last. Therefore, we should live life to the fullest each and every day, looking back only to learn and to see how far we've come while keeping our snouts pointed forward, to the future and what may lie ahead or around the corner.

I also learned it's important to be happy with oneself because life's too short to have too many unhappy days, and that one should pursue their dream today, rather than tomorrow. Paw-in paw with these lessons is the reality that the power to be happy and pursue dreams lies within me (and within each of us).

This realization led me to write "Ask Curtis" to help my fellow canines and other animals, including humans and cats, by providing dog-sense advice to address some of the issues getting in the way of their happiness.

Intended to be entertainingly informative, "Ask Curtis" contains letters seeking advice, which I answer in a sometimes serious, sometimes tongue-in-jowl manner.

So, sit back and enjoy yourself! If you're a dog find a nice cushy and warm place, turn around three times and lie down. If you're a human with a dog, lie down next to it — turning around is optional! If you're a cat,…oh well! And, if you feel the desire to ask Curtis for some dog-sense advice yourself, write away!!!

Barkingly yours,

Curtis the Dog

P.S. If you, your human or any other animal in your life, including cats, have any issues with which I can help, please email me at curtis@askcurtisthedog.com or write to me at the address listed on page 137!

LIST OF LETTER SENDERS

1. Moguls (Dog)

2. Emmett & Gibson (Dogs)

3. Cleo the Calico (Cat)

4. Terrified Terrier in Tulsa (Dog)

5. Wet & Wild in Wooster (Human)

6. Elder Speedster (Dog)

7. Misty Bell (Dog)

8. Treading Carefully in Agoura (Dog)

9. Chloe (Dog)

10. Born to be Free (Dog)

11. Kali (Dog)

12. Concerned in Connecticut (Human)

13. Murray the Mutt (Dog)

14. Phoebe (Cat)

15. What am I Thinking (Human)

16. Emmett (Dog)

17. Frisky and Lovin' It in Tarzana (Dog)

18. Zadie Don't Want Kids Afraidy (Human)

19. Blackie in the White Mountains (Dog)

20. Ellie Mae (AKA Predator) (Cat)

Picture of Curtis, courtesy of Matt Gersten

ASK CURTIS

Dear Curtis,

What gives with dogs wearing clothes? And, I'm not talking about some teeny-weenie, shorthaired dog, I'm talking about those of us a lot closer to our wolf ancestors. Why in the world are they wearing clothes? Come on now, White Fang wouldn't be caught dead wearing booties, a faux mink coat or pajamas! Pajamas?

I work under some pretty tough conditions as an Avalanche Dog at a ski resort and you won't find me wearing anything other than a vest that identifies me as a rescue dog. Well, maybe a bandana but that's because I look pretty rakish wearing one.

I just can't figure out how relatives of ours allow themselves to get so dolled up. And you should see some of the outfits them city dogs wear at the resort! For barking out loud! Why it ain't natural!

Curtis, why can't humans just leave us as we were meant to be and stop treating us like we're their kids? Clothes! What's this world coming to? It seems like it's gone to the humans!

Moguls (in the buff and proud of it!)

🐾 🐾 🐾

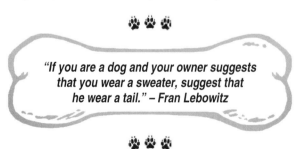

"If you are a dog and your owner suggests that you wear a sweater, suggest that he wear a tail." – Fran Lebowitz

🐾 🐾 🐾

Dear Moguls,

Try to understand that some of us are no longer limited to the region in which we were first bred and canines from hot climates are now living in cold ones — sort of like hot dogs freezing their buns off, so to bark!

And, while some dogs look to be farther from Grandma Wolf than do others of us, they're still our cousins despite being hairless or thin-haired, which makes them not as able to withstand temperatures and weather conditions as can you.

While you're fine with the cold, it's easy to imagine our cousins with smooth or minimal hair feeling cold when outside in chilly weather or damp when it's wet. Clothing, in the absence of a good natural fur coat, can make all the difference between a pleasant experience and an uncomfortably yucky one — and no one likes feeling uncomfortable, especially when relieving themselves. Plus, in all honesty, I know some "long-hairs" who appreciate feeling snug and extra warm when they go out into the cold as well.

Clothing also protects areas of our bodies that have been hurt, are vulnerable, or when we're assisting humans in areas having broken glass or other sharp objects like Ground Zero. Still other types of clothing are worn for safety like flotation vests and items with reflective devices when we're out at night.

Some clothing, however, does defy common dog-sense though I do understand why it's worn. While it has something to do with the dog, namely wanting to please its human, it has more to do with humans wanting their dogs to reflect themselves and their lifestyle.

T-shirts and tank tops with sayings on them, wristbands, bathrobes, dresses, tuxedos, pajamas, assorted jewelry and accessories, and costumes (except when it's Halloween) have little practical purpose and are generally fashion statements. And, some of our kind are "naturals" and hard for any human to resist dressing up, especially our "toy" cousins.

Moguls, what it comes down to is this — different togs for different dogs, and in your case, no togs. Even so, some say dressing us up is an extension of a human's love and isn't that what it's all about, being loved?

As for moi, I'm told I look pretty cool in my new shades when cruisin' the boulevard with the top down! See ya!

Curtis the Dog

TO WEAR & PROTECT

Aging dogs can benefit from some protection around their kidneys. Dogs who have been shaved or who have undergone medical treatments that result in the loss of fur will often need at least some temporary protection until their fur grows back.

DO CLOTHES MAKE THE DOG?

Popular & practical articles of clothing include:

- Coats, jackets and sweaters for the cold.
- Raincoats and slickers for wet weather.
- Booties for snow, ice, rain AND hot ground surfaces, or when in rugged terrain!
- Sunglasses or "Doggles" for eye protection.

Dear Curtis,

We're dogs right? We're known for eating everything we can, even stuff we're not supposed to eat, right? So, why, oh why, do we always get scolded for licking the dishes as they're being put in the dishwasher? Curtis, if they're gonna get cleaned anyway, what's the big "no" all about?

Confused,

Emmett and Gibson

(Note: Our two dishwashers can be found on page 67

Dear E&G,

I'm confused too! One of the occupations we're qualified for is "Dishwasher Extraordinaire" and some of us are bred to respond to the sound of a dishwasher door being opened by running into the kitchen, poking our heads into the machine's lower recesses and lapping the dishes. Your humans don't know how good they have it, especially when there are two of you!

It's certainly not because our saliva is unsanitary, and, besides, the dishes are dirty, for Canus' sake! Maybe they have young children whom they're afraid might adopt your dishwashing behavior. Personally, I feel it's never too early for humans to get their children to help around the house so what's the problem?

You know, until they prevent you from getting to the open dishwasher, go for it. Just remember – stay away from things with sharp serrated edges! Ouch!!!

Curtis the Dog

LICK ME AGAIN, SPARKY!
In a test done at the University of California, Davis, re-searchers found dog saliva killed E. coli and Strepto-coccus canis, another harmful bacteria.

DIRT CLEANS DISHES?
Some faiths believe that one's dishes, after having some of its contents lapped up by a dog, must be puri-fied by being washed seven times, one of which is with dirt!

Dear Curtis,

You're such a joke, acting like you know so much about everything. Ha! No way you even know half as much as my friends and I do. Dispensing advice to low-life dogs that can't climb trees or bring home something they killed...why, you and your kind can't even go out without being on a leash.

Curtis, why in the world would humans publish your book and not one from me?

Cleo the Calico

"Cat's Motto: No matter what you've done wrong, always make it look like the dog did it." - Unknown

"Cats are smarter than dogs. You will NEVER get eight cats to pull a sled through snow." - Jeff Valdez

Dear Cleo,

Am pleasantly surprised that a cat can read and write.

Yes, cats can climb trees. Big deal! Dogs can climb trees too but what's the point? Besides, when cats do it, it's usually because they're running away from us!

Yes, cats can bring home something they killed but only dogs are intelligent enough to bring home something that was already dead. And, while some of us have to wear a leash, no one calls us "scaredy dogs"!

As far as having humans publish my book and not one from you, guess it's because they realize that dogs really love them while cats only pretend. Don't you have a litter box waiting?

Curtis the Dog

"In order to keep a true perspective of one's importance, everyone should have a dog that will worship him and a cat that will ignore him." - Dereke Bruce, Taipei, Taiwan

Dear Curtis,

I'm a little adorable Yorkie and my mistress has gotten herself involved with a man who has an Irish Setter. For some reason they feel it's important for Finnegan and me to get along so whenever she spends time at his house, she brings me. Now there's really nothing wrong with Finnegan. I mean his breath is a little off-putting, but it's those really big paws, teeth and tongue. Quite honestly, I'd like nothing more than for my mistress to be happy but I'm petrified of Finnegan. He seems to be a friendly type of guy and I know he's been fixed yet I just can't get past his size. Curtis, what's a little dog to do?

Terrified Terrier in Tulsa.

Picture credit: Ingrid Müller & Marion Bugenings
Golightly Yorkshire-Terriers, Düsseldorf, Germany

Dear TT,

Abby, a little-dog friend of mine, went through a similar situation so I can identify with your plight.

For her, it worked out because she realized that all Frisco wanted to do was play. Wasn't his fault that his paws looked like sledgehammers and his panting felt like a hurricane. After being with him a few times, Abby realized that it was a matter of trust and that she had to overcome her fear of his size to appreciate his presence. And, she needed to realize that her master wouldn't be with someone who didn't have a nice dog.

My advice to her is the same as what I'm now expressing to you — give it some time and don't let your fear get in the way of a potential friendship. The true measure of a dog is the size of its heart and, from your description, Finnegan seems like a likeable fellow and probably just wants to play.

Curtis the Dog

PS. He doesn't drool or slobber, does he? If he does, that's a different story! Ick!

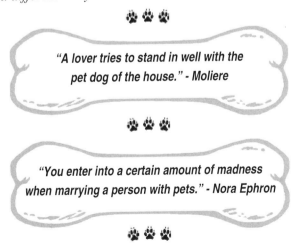

"A lover tries to stand in well with the pet dog of the house." - Moliere

"You enter into a certain amount of madness when marrying a person with pets." - Nora Ephron

Dear Curtis,

We've had a great Golden Retriever for several years. Vernon is a lot of fun and really enjoys going to our summer cottage with us. It's on a lake and we have a ski boat for our kids. Vernon loves going in the water and riding in the boat, especially when we go fast for water skiing.

Curtis, do you know of any Golden Retrievers who have learned how to use a ski board? We think Vernon could learn if we could show him a video or something.

Wet and Wild in Wooster

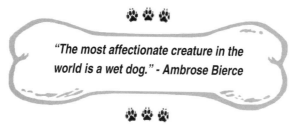

"The most affectionate creature in the world is a wet dog." - Ambrose Bierce

Dear W&W,

It's no surprise that Vernon has taken to the lake as many types of dogs love the water and Goldens are no exception. And, it's no surprise that he likes riding a fast boat because we like the fast moving vehicles that you humans use.

While not many dogs are hot-dogging it and I can't locate a video of us water skiing, don't be discouraged in training Vernon. Just start small.

Using a wake board or a training board for children, get Vernon to stand on the board, first on land, and then, in the lake with you holding it. Then, once he can balance himself on a "held" floating board, let go so he can find his balance on his own.

Once Vernon is comfortable standing on the board in the water, slowly move it for him to feel what it's like to stand on a moving board. Of course, as with any training, you'll need to reward him at various points along the way. Eventually, Vernon will let you know if he likes being on the board in the water and whether it's time to attach a rope tow to the board and give it a go. Please keep in mind that you will need to go slow as the nose of the board will go under water at a fast speed since Vernon can't pull the rope himself.

Hope I've helped and please let me know how Vernon does. As for moi, I'm a landlubber and the most excitement I have in the water is when I drink from the swimming pool!

Curtis the Dog

GET OUT OF THE WATER!
Developed for retrieving shot waterfowl along the Tweed River near Inverness, Scotland, Golden Retrievers' ancestry includes a number of water spaniels.

HOT DOGGING DOGS
A dog named Ducky uses a children's training board at a Belgian water ski club and two canine water sports enthusiasts, Keko and Roxy, have ridden the waves at a boat show in Marina del Rey, CA.

Dear Curtis,

I'm what you might call a senior citizen, being over 16 years old, and I've taken care of my family since I was a pup. It's been a good life but now I'm having a hard time seeing and my arthritis is killing me (especially typing this letter).

My back yard has rabbits, ground hogs, squirrels, chipmunks and other playmates whom I love to chase. Sadly, I can't run anymore so they just stand there when I come out to play and laugh. Curtis, what advice do you have on how to get "back up to speed?"

Elder Speedster

(Note: Elder Speedster can be found on page 67)

OH, MY ACHING BONES!
About 25-30% of pets suffer from osteoarthritis.

"Pay attention when an old dog is barking." - Proverb

GOOD FOR THEM, GOOD FOR US!
Arthritis remedies for canines contain glucosamine, or a combination of glucosamine/chondroitin, as do many of the products taken by people with arthritis.

Dear Elder Speedster,

Congratulations! Your 16 dog-years translates to about 80 human-years and that's quite an accomplishment for both a dog and a human! And, I'm thrilled you consider your life to have been a good one despite the relatively recent degradation of vision and the presence of arthritis as a daily companion.

If arthritis is truly bothering you, I'd get your humans to consult with your vet (if they haven't already) to see what type of arthritis you may have and whether there are medications or dietary changes that would help.

As far as your backyard playmates, looks like their last laugh is on you and that you might have to find some new tricks, which I know is not easy for an old(er) dog. So, if you can't chase them, outsmart them! Learn where their entry points are in the yard and stake them out, or find a way to make them come to you. Should that fail, perhaps it's best for you to accept and celebrate your stage in life. You've earned it and it may well be time to smell the roses rather than chase the rodents.

Curtis the Dog

🐾 🐾 🐾

"Every dog must have his day."
- Jonathan Swift

🐾 🐾 🐾

"In dog years I'm dead." - Unknown

🐾 🐾 🐾

Dear Curtis,

As a Beagle, I love to hunt rabbits and my instinct as a dog is to chase cats. At one time, I lived with Bunny, a very white & serious rabbit, and Kitty, an extremely black independent cat.

All three of us pets had a wonderful and peaceful time living with each other and we never said or did anything to hurt each other. Bunny would hop along and wiggle his nose and we, in turn, would touch noses to say hello. I do have to say that sometimes Kitty would take a swipe at me as I was walking by and I would chase her, but it was all in fun. Curtis, if a dog, cat and rabbit can live in harmony, why can't humans get along?

Misty Bell

"Dogs have not the power of comparing. A dog will take a small piece of meat as readily as a large, when both are before him." - Samuel Johnson

"If puss and dog can get together, why can't we love one another?" - Bob Marley

"Dogs have never hurt me. Only men have." - Marilyn Monroe

Dear Misty Bell,

The question why humans can't get along has been puzzling us since they were created – and don't forget we were here ahead of them and, thus, have observed them from their Beginning.

A wise old German Shepherd named Rinty once told me that ever since humans discovered that they came on the last day of Creation, they've been trying to be first and do not care what animals, including fellow humans, they have to step on, enslave, abuse, bully or kill to get there.

Another canine sage, a bulldog named Lombardi, says it's because humans aren't team players despite their fascination with team sports. He says it has something to do with how many humans are born per birth occasion. While the incidence of multiple humans per birth occasion is rare (unless a fertility drug is involved), that's not the case with us. So, humans don't learn how to share as soon after they're whelped as do we. After all, nothing teaches you about sharing and patience than having to wait with your womb-mates for an available teat.

Still, a wise ol' hound named Barney told me it has to do with the fact that humans wear clothes while we don't. I find this especially interesting given Rinty barking that some humans believe that in their distant past they were butt naked in some garden and that all was wonderful and edenic at that time. Then, it's told, they did something that forced them to wear clothes and, since then, it's been anything but peaceful. Getting back to clothes, if humans were naked, there wouldn't be any wars since they wouldn't be able to tell who was on what side without uniforms!

A scrappy little terrier named Jack Russell says it has to do with the "two P's": Possessions and Power. Sure, we have pecking orders, territorial disagreements, peeing contests, head-butts, and even wars, but humans have taken it to a higher degree. I mean, when was the last time you saw an army ant in a tank or Humvee? Jack went on to tell me that when he was obtained from his breeder, a couple of human families both wanted him and almost came to blows over it! Amazing!

So, Misty Bell, whatever the reason, humans haven't as yet learned how to play nice with one another and share their toys. Guess in this human-eat-human world, us lower intelligent members of the Animal Kingdom still have some educating to do with people who think they're Nature's royalty! Meanwhile, I have to go. Seems I hear my master and his teenage son having a disagreement — something about cleaning up a room and I might need to referee!

Curtis the Dog

IT'S CROWDED IN HERE!

The average female dog has 6-9 puppies per litter, the average female domestic cat has 4-6 kittens per litter, and female rabbits, depending on their type, have 3-8 bunnies per litter.

"If you pick up a starving dog and make him prosperous, he will not bite you; that is the principal difference between a dog and a man." - Mark Twain

"Dogs are our link to paradise. They don't know evil or jealousy or discontent. To sit with a dog on a hillside on a glorious afternoon is to be back in Eden, where doing nothing was not boring — it was peace." - Milan Kundera

"Dogs love their friends and bite their enemies, quite unlike people, who are incapable of pure love and always have to mix love and hate in their object-relations." - Sigmund Freud

"The only creatures that are evolved enough to convey pure love are dogs and infants." - Johnny Depp

Dear Curtis,

My master and those of some of my friends do not pick up after us. Why, the mess in my neighborhood has gotten so bad that even I don't like to be walked. It's not that we can do anything about it, after all a dog's gotta do what a dog's gotta do and it's not like we can pick up after ourselves.

The town I live in is installing mutt mitt dispensers and waste baskets as if that's going to get my irresponsible master and others like him to take the initiative to pick up after us. Curtis, help! I'm almost up to my hock joint in poop!

Treading Carefully in Agoura.

Picture courtesy of The Casual Canine, San Diego, CA,
www.casualcanine.com

Dear Treading!

Reading your letter, my initial reaction was to get angry with you and your friends for allowing your owners to be so badly mannered and inconsiderate of their fellow humans. After all, if we dogs can't train our masters to respect their neighbors and the environment by picking up after us, how in the world can we expect global peace where everyone has their own hydrant and steak-bone?

So here's a suggestion. The next time your owner allows you to poop on someone else's lawn or along the street where human adults and children might walk, run, bike or play and doesn't pick it up... roll in it and rub yourself along your master's leg, giving him or her the biggest, cutest, happiest and lovingest dog smile you can!!! And keep doing it until he gets the message to clean up after you!

Curtis the Dog

"Dogs need to sniff the ground; it's how they keep abreast of current events. The ground is a giant dog newspaper, containing all kinds of late-breaking dog news items, which, if urgent, are often continued in the next yard." - Dave Barry

Dear Curtis,

I have a favorite thing, with which my companions have a problem. They used to let me run off-leash because I am very well behaved and always have her or him in sight (I don't want them to lose me) but now, they almost never let me off-leash.

I think it's because my next most favorite thing after running off-leash is to roll in another dog's poop and because every time that I ran back to them for a hug after a good roll, they got really angry, yelled at me and immediately gave me a shower. Curtis, how can I convince them that rolling in poop is a pleasure that all should enjoy?

Chloe

(Note: Chloe can be found on page 67)

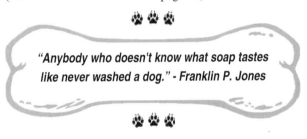

"Anybody who doesn't know what soap tastes like never washed a dog." - Franklin P. Jones

Rollin' in the Poop!!!

Dear Chloe,

Ah, the ol' roll-in-the-poop maneuver!

The interesting thing is that rolling in poop is a relatively common canine behavior that goes back to our wolf-pack days when we needed to disguise our scent to sneak up on prey. Of course, some of us doo-bathe because we don't like the way we smell or, simply, because we like to smell crappy. Actually, I had a big-roller poodle friend do it so often that her owners referred to her as a "Stink-a-doodle."

While "rolling in it" may be a perfectly acceptable behavior in our world, humans have this compulsion to be clean and an aversion to most things that smell stinky, including the soiled diapers of their young! (You wanna talk stinky? Please pass the nose clips!)

Humans also suffer long-term memory loss and don't remember when they lived with us in the caves and rolled in the stuff themselves. After all, aren't some fragrances called toilet water?

So it looks like you're not going to convince your companions that poop rolling is a pleasurable activity in which they, themselves, should partake. And, it looks like you're confined to the length of your leash until further notice or until wintertime when poop freezes over! As for moi, I prefer a roll in the hay to a roll in the poop most anytime!

Curtis the Dog

Dear Curtis,

I've been with my family for as long as I can remember but, since I'm only a year old, there's not that much to remember. Anyway, we have a lot of fun playing together and I try to be a good companion. I have my own living area in the house (my family calls it "the cage") complete with a comfortable cushion and a water bowl with my name on it. It's great for napping while the family is away but there's a door on it, and whenever the family doesn't want me around, like when they're eating, they put me in there and close the door.

Curtis, do you have any ideas on how to stay out of the cage at dinnertime?

Born To Be Free

Dear BTBF,

Some humans welcome us to the dinner table and some do not. Some humans share their food with us and some find this behavior distasteful. Whether we're allowed near the table during a human meal largely depends on how we behave (whether food is shared with us or not), and whether it's okay with our humans to have a wet nose poking their leg under the table or a pair of deep brown eyes pitifully staring up at them as they try to enjoy a meal.

Obviously, the most foolproof anti-begging solution is to restrict you from the kitchen or dining area during meals and that appears to be what your humans are doing by caging you.

Hopefully, with attentive humans who can follow the anti-begging tips I've listed below and good behavior on your part, you will obtain your freedom at dinnertime. Keeping it though will be another story because you'll really have to discipline yourself, something which we dogs, like some people, are not very good at when it comes to food. As for moi, I've learned that patience works wonders and I'm a lucky dog to have a sharing human.

Curtis the Dog

"No animal should ever jump up on the dining-room furniture unless absolutely certain that he can hold his own in the conversation." - Fran Lebowitz

ANTI-BEGGING TIPS

- Feed the dog before feeding yourself.
- No reinforcement or reward, so no food from the table and no surprise dropping from plate-to-floor.
- Train the dog to obey the "down stay" command and give it away from the table (or in another room).
- Offer all dog treats away from the table, in its food bowl for example, to avoid any association the dog might make between treats and the dinner table.

"Never trust a dog to guard your food."
- Anonymous

"My dog, she looks at me sometimes with that look, and I think maybe deep down inside she must know exactly how I feel. But then maybe she just wants the food off my plate." - Anonymous

DEN AND NOW

Dogs have retained a denning instinct from their "early wild days," which can be seen when they lie down under desks and tables or when they dig in the yard. Today's dens, which take the form of dog houses, crates and cages provide a place of refuge when they're tired, stressed or just looking to get away from it all. From a human perspective, they also are places to put a dog when you want to protect your house from real or imagined dog-related destruction, facilitate a dog's travel, especially by car or plane, have a place to send a dog when you feel it needs a time-out or when you just don't want to be bothered by a dog's presence, e.g., when having company or at dinnertime.

Dear Curtis,

I'm a 2-year old female Husky and my best friend is Nikki. He's also a Husky, but he's, like, old...somewhere around 15 or 16. Before he goes to doggie heaven, our owners would like us to mate but, because Nikki is too old to do it the ol' fashioned way, they took us to some doctor to try to do it artificially. Not very romantic if you ask me and it didn't work. Now they want to do it again.

Curtis, should I be flattered? I mean, yeah, if anyone is gonna knock me up, I'd like it to be Nikki...but is it wrong to at least ask for a little Barry White music the next time?

Love,

Kali

P.S. You're a Golden mix, otherwise I'd ask you to "dad" my pups.

Dear Kali,

I'm flattered that you would consider me to sire your puppies though, separate and aside from the fact that I'm not a Husky, I no longer have the capability of producing pupsters. Besides, you like Nikki. He's your best friend and your choice to impregnate you, even if he can no longer do it doggy-style.

The reality is that Nikki must have some good Husky qualities in addition to some good dog ones. Just the fact that he's made it to his age is a testament to good genes, not taking anything away from the care and love he must have received. So, as the song goes, it's back to "doing what comes artificially."

Supposedly there are artificial insemination (AI) methods

that increase the odds of your becoming pregnant and I hope your doctor is using one because I don't think you'd want to go through the procedure a third time, even if they did play Barry White!

Kali, my advice is for you to make the best of the situation even though there's no romantic music, red roses or mood lighting. And, if all goes well this time around, in about nine weeks after the procedure, you and Nikki should be the proud parents of pupsters and I'll venture to say that how they were conceived will be a wonderful story to tell your grandpuppies!

Curtis the Dog

ADVANTAGES OF AI

- **Eliminates risk of injury from an uncooperative or overly cooperative partner.**
- **Avoids fright or fatigue from "doing it" naturally.**
- **Can check semen quality for color, infection and motility & numbers with inexpensive microscope.**
- **Good when a stud dog is deceased, geographically undesirable, or doesn't regularly "tie-one-on."**
- **Dog doesn't lose natural mating instinct or ability.**
- **Pups are still recognized by AKC if certified vet used as well as an officially sanctioned collection and storage facility for canine semen.**

Dear Curtis,

I'm the proud mistress of a red Standard Poodle named Nicki. She's about 7 years old and 42 pounds. I recently brought home donuts and left them on the table, but pushed back from the edge as Nicki can rest her nose on it and we all know better than to leave anything near the edge just in case. Nicki must have been very hungry, or simply lost all her will power, as she jumped up and stole a chocolate donut. I had just walked in from the garage to see her devour the last crumb.

I know dogs shouldn't eat chocolate and worried that she would be sick for the next 24 hours but she never threw up or seemed to experience any ill effects. Curtis, how serious a problem is eating chocolate and what should I have done?

Concerned in Connecticut

(Note: Nicki can be found on page 68)

Dear CC,

Dogs and chocolate shouldn't mix unless we're talking about a Chocolate Labrador. It can lead to cardiac arrhythmias and seizures, particularly if the pooch is prone to epilepsy or has become overly excited – and what dog wouldn't be excited after wolfing down some Godiva?

Whether chocolate is fatal depends on the dog's size and type of chocolate and Nicki, at 42 pounds, would need to have eaten a lot more chocolate than what's in one donut to have gotten into doggy-heaven.

Even so, you should take steps to protect Nikki from herself by keeping any unsweetened baking chocolate in closed containers in upper cupboards and milk chocolate well out of her reach. Also, you'll need to be strong and never give chocolate to her despite the sad looks and loud whimpers.

Finally, be especially careful around holiday times when chocolate candy is out-and-about and all too available and tempting. Personally, Halloween is one of my favorite times and this year I went as Spiderdog!

Curtis the Dog

IT'S A KILLER (PERHAPS)
Chocolate contains a caffeine-like compound called theobromine, which can be fatal to dogs.

SIZE OF DOG/TYPE OF CHOCOLATE
A killer serving is approximately 1 oz. of milk chocolate, 1/3 oz. of semisweet chocolate, or 1/10 oz. of baker's chocolate per pound of dog.

EARLY SIGNS OF CHOCOLATE POISONING
The first signs of chocolate poisoning are usually vomiting, diarrhea, increased urination and nausea, which can progress to cardiac arrhythmias and seizures, particularly if the pooch is prone to epilepsy or has become overly excited.

WHAT TO DO, WHAT TO DO?
- Induce vomiting — stick your fingers down the dog's throat or give it a solution of ½ hydrogen peroxide and ½ water.
- Call your vet, who may tell you to bring the dog in immediately.
  - If possible, bring any unfinished chocolate with you to help the vet appropriately treat the dog.

BURN THAT TOAST!
Activated charcoal or extremely black burnt toast will chemically bond with ingested chocolate allowing it to be safely eliminated by the dog.

Dear Curtis,

Back in February, my owners ended their 5-year relationship. It was very sad and an adjustment had to be made by all. After the split, I began living mostly with dad Grant, but mom Leslie would get to see me every other weekend, mostly when she was with her 11-year old son, and my buddy, Robby.

While this has been working out fine for several months, I'm starting to get sick of the back-and-forth travel. I really like the swinging bachelor pad that dad has created for me and now, more and more, I find myself getting sad as the weekend with mom approaches. Plus, there's a really hot Beagle that lives across the street that I'm just getting to know.

Curtis, how do I show my owners that I'm done with this custody sharing and that I want to stay put? Should I start being bad while I'm at mom's house...say pee on the floor and eat wallpaper? Please help!

Murray the Mutt

(Note: Murray can be found on page 68)

Dear Murray,

You're not alone. Like children, dogs are negatively impacted by the fact that humans have difficulty loving and living with one another over time.

After all, we're social animals and tend to bond to a "family" routine and way of life. Thus, when our "family" dissolves, our world usually dissolves as well and some of us, especially if we're old enough to have stopped learning new tricks, may have a hard time adjusting to the change, which could involve being shuttled between parents much like some children.

I must say that you appear to have adjusted well to your parents' breakup and until recently were happy with the back-and-forth travel. Now that you have this swinging bachelor pad and have met a hot Beagle (which may not be as good as a hot bagel), I can understand why you no longer wish to mimic a tug toy. Oftentimes, as a child of divorce gets older, their social life increases causing them to cut back on spending time with one of their parents. This appears to be happening with you.

So, what to do? Destroying property is not an answer so peeing on your mom's floor and eating wallpaper, unless it's liver-flavored, isn't a way to go...and it can make your mouth really pasty. Perhaps your parents will understand how you feel if you refuse to get into your mom's car when she picks you up. Or, try hiding. As a last resort, howl when you get to your mom's and keep howling until she returns you to your dad. Hopefully, after a few visits with you howling and her not sleeping well, both she and your dad will get it.

Curtis the Dog

Dear Curtis,

I hope you take requests from cats as there's something on my mind. My companions like to go away on weekends and take me with them (as well as the dog though I can't understand why).

Although I don't really mind the car trips, and being in VT is not so bad (they don't let me out of the house there but at least there are mice!), I do not like to make the transition from house-to-car. I can always tell when they are getting ready to travel: bags always appear at the bottom of the stairs and they yell a lot. I always hang around in sight until just moments before they are ready to leave and then, I hide.

My problem is that I am running out of hiding places since I never reuse a hiding place once it has been discovered. Don't bother suggesting under the radiator, inside an old box spring, inside a closet, between sheets or sweaters, or under a chair or sofa because I've used them all. Curtis, what's a cat to do?

Sincerely,

Phoebe

(Note: Phoebe can be found on page 68)

Dear Phoebe,

Let me get this straight, you don't mind trips by car, you mind trips from the house to the car! Ain't that just like a cat?

Okay, is there something about the trip from the house to the car that you don't like? Do they pick you up by the scruff of the neck and carry you a relatively long distance to the car? Do they carry you in their arms so tightly that you feel as if you're suffocat-

ing and going to pass out? Do they carry you on their shoulder like a Continental soldier? Or do they hold you so close you can smell their bad breath?

Ah, what to do, what to do? Well, you can... GET OVER IT! Though I don't know any cat shrinks, I can make inquiries. However, I don't believe that there are any, or at least any that are good, since all the cats I know are so screwed up...oops, sorry, forgot my manners – again.

Since therapy's out of the question, here are two suggestions. Most cats I know love going in and out of a paper shopping bag so, just before you're taken to the car, find one and crawl into it. Then, all they have to do is carry you to the car in it! Kind of brings new meaning to the phrase "it's in the bag," don't you think? Otherwise, hide in the car! They'll never, ever, look for you there! Hope I've helped, you rotten...oops, sorry!

Curtis the Dog

🐾 🐾 🐾

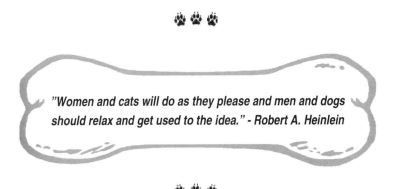

"Women and cats will do as they please and men and dogs should relax and get used to the idea." - Robert A. Heinlein

🐾 🐾 🐾

Dear Curtis,

I'm a thirty-something single male with a 9-to-5-office job. I'm seriously considering getting a puppy. It would be my first dog ever so I don't have the slightest clue on raising one. I've also heard horror stories from others and I'm wondering whether I have the wherewithal and time that would be needed to train and bring a puppy up in a caring and loving manner. Curtis, you think, perhaps, I should get an older dog?

What Am I Thinking?

Dear Thinking,

You're asking the right question. Now you have to answer whether you can honestly provide what a puppy (or dog) needs.

It takes a lot of work and plenty of time to teach a puppy all the things it needs to know to be a fun, healthy, happy dog. Average adult dogs, such as moi, need you to play with us, exercise us, teach us good manners (though we could teach you a few things about manners), groom us, feed and water us and let us relieve ourselves. Count on at least half an hour every morning and an hour every evening (though my old friend Rusty sometimes takes forever just to lift his leg!). And puppies take more time than older dogs. In fact, the younger the dog the more time you have to add. For very young puppies you will want to take them out about every two hours and that's one reason why busy people (did I read 9-to-5 job?) often start with an adult dog.

And, how are you with babies? Puppies are babies and they will do things that make you mad just because they are learning. And, as they grow up, they act like teenagers (yikes!) and try to get away with doing what they want, instead of what you want. While being firm is okay, getting angry is useless and can make things worse.

Also, dogs don't speak human and until humans learn to speak dog, we'll just have to keep trying to understand you. So you will need to say what you mean and mean what you say. For example, does "sit" really mean "sit" or "sit if you want to"?

Lastly, before getting a puppy (or an older dog), ask yourself, do you have trouble getting all your chores done without being reminded? If so, it might not yet be time for you to get a dog. Having a dog is a responsibility, and remember that the words in "what am I thinking?" start with the letters W-A-I-T!

Curtis the Dog

🐾 🐾 🐾

"Whoever said you can't buy happiness forgot about little puppies." - Gene Hill

🐾 🐾 🐾

"No matter how little money and how few possessions you own, having a dog makes you rich." - Louis Sabin

🐾 🐾 🐾

Dear Curtis,

I live in Boston and, every winter, look forward to the first snowfall and to getting my gold fur all covered in white. I run around my yard for hours and make snow angels but, sometimes, I get bored and turn to poopsicles. This is extremely "irritating" to my owners, who go on and on about how it's not sanitary, blah, blah, blah. Frankly, I don't care. After all, nothing's better than some good ol' frozen droppings to spice up an afternoon.

To stop this behavior, my owner now picks up after me so that there are no snacks for later. Bummer. Curtis, is there anything I can tell my parents to convince them it's all in a good day's fun? Plus, think of all the money they'd save on dog treats if they'd just let me do my "doo-ty"?!? Have you ever tried one?

Emmett, a Golden hoping to have his doo and eat it too.

(Note: Emmett can be found on page 69)

SCAVENGERS AT THE GATE!
Some believe feces-eating, or coprophagia, is caused by poor diet or poor health. Others attribute it to the fact that dogs are historically scavengers and that chowing down on poop is a scavenger behavior.

Dear Emmett,

Some dogs can't resist a tasty morsel of feces, whether it's from horses, cats, other animals, human babies, other dogs or themselves, and frozen feces are a popular "treat" in wintertime.

For most humans, feces-eating is pretty disgusting, particu-

larly if we throw the consumed crap up on their carpet, bedspread or child. Wow, bark about disgusting! Further, it exposes us to parasites and diseases even if it's our own that we're eating. Ick!

If you're unable to convince your owners to save some poopsicles for you, get them to make other frozen treats, which you can enjoy throughout the year and not just in the wintertime.

If you still insist on eating frozen poop, do it when your owners aren't looking, wipe that poop-eating grin off your face and take a doggy-mint. As for moi, I'll be content never to see a snow-flake and to digest my food only once.

Curtis the Dog

P.S. If you're eating feces to relieve boredom, read a book instead!

BLAME IT ON MOM
Eating feces is normal for a mother dog from whom her pups learn the behavior, much as human children learn some undesirable behaviors from their moms. Most pups stop eating poop once they are weaned.

FROZEN TREATS ALL YEAR ROUND
There are many tasty frozen dog treats you can make with yogurt mixed with carrots, apples, cooked ground liver, tuna, and pumpkin to name a few.

"The great pleasure of a dog is that you may make a fool of yourself with him, and not only will he not scold you, but he will make a fool of himself too." - Samuel Butler

Dear Curtis,

My name is Coco and I'm an adorable little Pomeranian, or so I've been told. My owners feel I have a problem of an addictive nature and are threatening to take away something of mine that I hold dear. The fact that they feel this way is causing me much anxiety and I'm having a lot of negative thoughts towards them. Don't get me wrong as I adore my family and lick them to death but, the way I see it, they're the ones with the problem, not me.

It's all about the plush stuffed toy bone I was given as a pup. It's filthy, cuddly, has a wonderful shape and I can't get enough of it. I like to throw it in the air and have it land on my back, shake it from side-to-side until I'm dizzy, fetch it when someone is kind enough to throw it and I especially like to do this little dance with it that makes me feel really, really good if you know what I mean. Apparently, my family has a problem with the latter and refers to it as humping, not dancing. Further, they seem quite uncomfortable and down right embarrassed with my behavior when they have company.

Humping?? Frankly, I'm insulted and hurt. All I'm doing is playing with my bone. If I get a little pleasure at the same time, why should they get so bent out of shape to make me feel like I'm doing something shameful? Come on, it's not like I drink out of the toilet or chew on their underwear! By the way, I could write a book about some of the things I've witnessed while on my owners' bed at night and they don't seem to care whether I'm embarrassed or even notice that I exist at that point. Actually, truth be told, I find it pretty interesting and enjoyable to watch.

Bottom line is that they are thinking about getting rid of my bone if I don't change my behavior. Don't they realize how much I love and need it? Curtis what should I do? How can I make my family understand that my behavior is perfectly okay and that they need to be a bit more open minded?

Lots of licks,

Frisky and Lovin' It In Tarzana

(Note: Coco can be found on page 70)

"I think we are drawn to dogs because they are the uninhibited creatures we might be if we weren't certain we knew better." - George Bird Evans

"Shallow, phony patriotism will always draw a crowd, like dogs humping in the street." - Keith Olbermann

Dear Coco,

Like dancing with your bone, do you? Whether it's dancing or humping, your behavior toward your plush stuffed toy is upsetting to your owners. Too bad they can't appreciate the fact that you're not doing it with a human appendage, or that all you might be doing is just showing your toy who's boss!

So, given that you don't wish to part with your toy, what should you do? Perhaps you can get your owner to wash it. Therefore, when you next see them ready to do a wash, slip the toy into the hamper! Washing the toy might remove their perception that the toy itself is disgusting, and a clean toy might not have as stimulating a smell to you as it might now have.

You might also stop dancing when asked. To continue pelvic thrusting after being asked to cease-and-desist is like pouring gasoline on fire and only serves to make your owners more determined to rid you of your habit by ridding you of your toy. Besides, there'll always be opportunities to dance when no one is looking.

Coco, if you want to keep your toy, you need to be mindful of your activity with it. Throwing it in the air, having it land on your back, shaking it from side-to-side until you're dizzy and fetching it are all cute and acceptable behaviors. Doing your dance is not and should be kept private, even if it's just your owners that are around. If you persist in publicly dancing, by all means, wipe that glazed look off your muzzle and don't light up a cigarette afterwards!

Curtis the Dog

"It is fatal to let any dog know that he is funny, or he immediately loses his head and starts hamming it up." - P.G. Woodehouse

SAVE THE LAST HUMP FOR ME!

While much of the humping one sees among puppies as well as among adult dogs is play, some of it expresses dominance. Other reasons for humping may have to do with an irritation or itching in the genital area as well as sexual arousal. Usually when a female is in heat, she, other females and, of course, the males around her may well turn into humping fools. Sometimes having a dog neutered or a medical condition corrected may "cure" the dog from humping, but not if it's become a habit.

"Little Joe Dirt: Can I push him off of me?
Miss Clipper: He'll stop humping as soon as he's done." - From the Movie "Joe Dirt"

Dear Curtis:

I have a 9-year old daughter and a 5-year old granddaughter both of whom are fearful of dogs. Once my 9-year old gets to know a dog she usually warms up to it but it is difficult to get her to hang out with a dog long enough to get to that point. My granddaughter will go out of her way to avoid dogs and, oftentimes, when approaching a dog, she'll freak out and get whomever is with her to cross the street so as not to pass it.

I want both my daughter and granddaughter to know the joy that a friendship with dogs can bring but there is little chance of ever having a dog in the family since both my wife and my granddaughter's mother are not pet people. Curtis, any advice you can give will be most helpful.

Sincerely,

Zadie, Don't Want Kids Afraidy

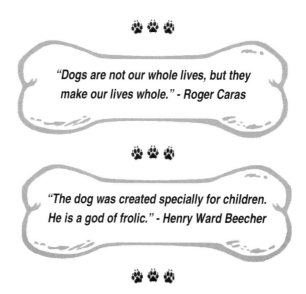

🐾 🐾 🐾

"Dogs are not our whole lives, but they make our lives whole." - Roger Caras

🐾 🐾 🐾

"The dog was created specially for children. He is a god of frolic." - Henry Ward Beecher

🐾 🐾 🐾

Dear Zadie,

It is not uncommon for your daughter and, especially, your granddaughter to feel as they do because a top fear children experience is the fear of animals, most often dogs.

To help your daughter and granddaughter overcome their fear, you will need to both acknowledge their anxiety and help them get comfortable with my kind. It will take some time and it won't be easy, so you'll need to be persistent in a supportive and positive way. Hopefully, some of the tips on page 49 might be of help.

The good news is that most children who are fearful of dogs outgrow their apprehension. Interestingly, fear-of-dogs in adults can often stem from a lack of exposure to dogs when they, themselves, were young; an unfounded fear that's been carried for far too long.

We dogs can usually tell when a person is fearful of us and we can usually tell when a person just doesn't like us. How upsetting! Especially when you consider that most of my kind are designed to do nothing but please people. And, what's not to like?

It truly would be a shame if your daughter and granddaughter carried "inherited" fears, which prevented them from enjoying the love, friendship and companionship that we, one of the true natural wonders of the world, provide. With your help though, the odds of that happening will be significantly reduced.

Zadie, that was the more complicated answer. The simple answer is a five-letter word....PUPPY!!!

Curtis the Dog

> *"If you don't own a dog, at least one, there is not necessarily anything wrong with you, but there may be something wrong with your life."* - Roger Caras

HOW DOES A CHILD LEARN TO FEAR DOGS?

- By experiencing or witnessing a real dog attack.

- By having a large dog run toward them.

- By the dog itself, complete with loud noises, paws, tail, slobber, licking and exuberant behavior, like jumping, that can easily be mistaken as being harmful.

- By a fear-of-dogs that others have, especially if they are parents, an older sibling or a friend.

TIPS TO OVERCOMING A CHILD'S FEAR

- Don't push them to face their fears or try to convince them that there isn't any reason to be afraid.
- Don't judge them for being afraid or belittle them.
- Don't force them to pet a dog they don't want to pet.
- Teach them to enjoy happy-go-lucky, fun-loving canines as well as to keep a healthy distance from strange dogs whose behavior and temperament may be unpredictable.
- Be straightforward in explaining that dogs are like people and when they feel threatened by someone they don't know getting too close or looking at them too hard or too long, they can react by barking, growling, chasing, or even nipping.
- Point out pooches on walks together and read stories or watch videos about good-natured dogs and their happy owners.
- Visit a pet store to see adorable, penned puppies at a safe distance, which will help them feel in control.
- Introduce them to a friend's or neighbor's dog, and show them how to talk to and pet it to get a positive response.

Dear Curtis,

Joey, my Beagle buddy, was abducted by U.S. Customs and now is sniffing the legs of people who haven't taken showers for many hours while traveling on airplanes to Dulles airport. What makes matters worse, whenever he makes a score and sniffs out some old lady's stash, he can't even get a hit of the spoils! All he gets is a stinking milk bone! Now I wake up in the middle of the night half-scared to death that I will be abducted by Customs! Curtis, what should I do?

Blackie in the White Mountains

"I have a great dog. She's half Lab, half pit bull. A good combination. Sure, she might bite off my leg, but she'll bring it back to me." - Jimi Celeste

Dear Blackie,

I don't believe you have the entire story straight. To begin with, detector dogs lead an interesting life and it's a terrific opportunity for us canines to serve our country. And, seeing as most detector dogs are obtained from animal shelters, I doubt that Joey was abducted. Why, he may have volunteered!

As a member of "The Beagle Brigade," Joey is helping U.S. farmers safeguard their crops and animals by detecting meats and produce that are banned from crossing our country's borders. He is well fed, given the best of veterinary care, and will remain on the job until age or infirmity makes him incapable of dogging his post. Then, he'll be eased into a well-deserved retirement, most likely being adopted by his handler.

So, Blackie, I wouldn't worry about Joey if I were you. He's having fun, being well fed and attended, is with a caring human partner and he's helping his country. And, I wouldn't lose any sleep worrying that I might be abducted by Customs either. Besides, if you're like me, you might look pretty good in a uniform. I've heard it's a good way to meet the ladies. Hey, feel like enlisting with me?

Curtis the Dog

SERVING OUR COUNTRY!!!
Since 1970, the Customs Service has been using dogs to search for narcotics and dangerous drugs and, relatively recently, detector dogs have been used to sniff out currency as well as chemical weapons.

"Dogs like to obey. It gives them security."
- James Herriot

FROM WHERE DO SNIFFERS COME?
While a breeding program supplies some dogs, and a small percentage are donated by their owners, approximately 80 percent of U.S. Customs' sniffing specialists come from a network of animal shelters.

An instructor at the Customs and Border Protection Canine Enforcement Training Center demonstrates the abilities of a chemical detection dog. Photograph courtesy Gerald L. Nino/U.S. Customs

AND, THE IDEAL CANDIDATE IS...

- Mostly hunters and workers including Labs and Goldens, German Shepherds, Brittany Spaniels, German Short-Hairs, Belgian Malinois and mixed breeds.
- A male or female from one-to-three years of age.
- Has an outgoing, curious personality.
- Is able to remain calm and focused around loud noises and chaotic situations like border-crossing traffic or airport crowds.
- Is passionate about retrieving, i.e., becomes totally excited by retrieving and retrieves anything for any-one, anywhere, anytime without tiring.

CHARGE OF "THE BEAGLE BRIGADE"

- Over 60 teams.
- U.S. Department of Agriculture (USDA).
- Works in over 20 international airports across the United States.
- Forms a critical barrier against the entry of plant and animal diseases into the U.S.
- Sniffs out and confiscates an average of 75,000 prohibited fruits, vegetables, and meats a year.

Dear Curtis,

Last year, I was adopted by my human who gave me a wonderful home. However, after a couple of months, she went into a hospital and during that time, while other people looked after me, I became a wild, misbehaving kitty. Though my human is back living with me and I feel loved, I'm more spoiled and basically control the household. I stalk, spit and hiss at visitors and I bite and claw whenever I feel like it. The vet says that I'm not socialized. Curtis, is there any help for me? Can I change and become a nice kitty? I'd like to make my human proud of me.

Ellie Mae (AKA Predator)

(Note: Ellie Mae can be found on page 71)

"It's easy to understand why the cat has eclipsed the dog as modern America's favorite pet. People like pets to possess the same qualities they do. Cats are irresponsible and recognize no authority, yet are completely dependent on others for their material needs. Cats cannot be made to do anything useful. Cats are mean for the fun of it." - P.J. O'Rourke

Dear Ellie Mae,

My sympathy to those who have to be in contact with you. Your letter suggests that prior to your human going into a hospital, you might have been a better behaving cat than you are now. If this is true, the "good kitty" is in your DNA, which makes your nasty self-centered feline behavior even more despicable since the only thing preventing you from being nice is YOU!

Assuming your stalking, spitting, hissing, biting and clawing is in response to anxieties or insecurities caused by inconsistent care-giving and the loss of a wonderful home when your human was hospitalized, that is no longer the case and you now have the ability to modify your rotten defensive behavior. So....GET OVER IT! That you continue to act out implies you need a shrink and not a vet who, by the way, was kind in saying you're not socialized. I'm not as kind.

You say you want to make your human proud of you and then make her anything but proud. Now, ain't that just like a cat?! You want to make her proud? Stop thinking just about yourself for a change! This isn't about you. Be nice! Start acting like a dog!

Curtis the Dog

🐾 🐾 🐾

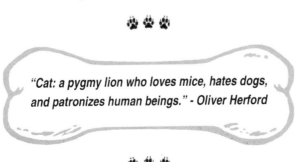

"Cat: a pygmy lion who loves mice, hates dogs, and patronizes human beings." - Oliver Herford

🐾 🐾 🐾

Dear Curtis,

My daughter owns two dogs. A wolf mix who weighs about 120 pounds named Fang, and a Great Dane named Hans, who must be at least 165 pounds. Her boyfriend's small, but loud and yappy dog, Melvin, also frequents her house and now she has "rescued" two apparently abandoned dogs.

So, Curtis, why at the age of 30 is she so immature? And why does she continue to do everything she can to make my wife and me miserable? Why can't these dogs teach her to grow up?

Mystified in Mystic

Dear Mystified,

Dogs have a limited vocabulary so every one of our words has a clear and concise meaning. As such we have no need for a dictionary like you humans. Even so, I consulted one and learned that immature means "lacking complete growth, differentiation, or development." It also means, "having the potential capacity to attain a definitive form or state" as well as "exhibiting less than an expected degree of maturity."

Based on this, common dog-sense suggests that your expectations of your daughter's maturity may in itself be premature. Further, there's probably still time for her to attain her potential.

Over the years, I've known some mature dogs with terrible dispositions and some rather immature ones who were happy just to have some kibble, a dry bed and an occasional ear scratch. So, you might want to ask yourself if your daughter is happy, regardless of how mature you presently judge her to be.

As for her making you and your wife miserable, I've learned that no matter how I tilt my head or sad I make my eyes, I can't make my master feel guilty about not giving me table scraps unless he allows it. Therefore, feeling miserable has more to do with how you respond to your daughter's behavior (or your expectations of it) than anything else.

Her affinity with my species suggests a high capacity to love and be responsible. While you question why the dogs in her life can't teach her to grow up, we canines know that we don't teach your kind about growing up, just about playing nice! After all, we don't live for very long in human terms and so we try to stay a puppy for as long as we can. Perhaps your daughter's trying to do the same thing. I've heard it said that life begins at 40-human years. You indicate she's 30. Cheer up, there's still time.

Curtis the Dog

P.S. For what it's worth, some say my late 50-ish master hasn't grown up yet!!!

"He is your friend, your partner, your defender, your dog. You are his life, his love, his leader. He will be yours, faithful and true, to the last beat of his heart. You owe it to him to be worthy of such devotion." - Unknown

Dear Curtis,

Bet you never thought you'd hear from me. I'm a Ctenocephalides canis and my kind and I love to get under your skin. Well, not really under your skin as we prefer to live on you and your kind, nourishing ourselves, frolicking around, raising our families and, in the process, making you one itchy, unhappy and potentially sick dog.

The problem is that my family and I have been out of circulation for a while and have forgotten what it's like to live on a dog. See, for the past year, we've been headlining at Fleadomland Circus where working conditions were awful. So, goodbye cruel circus, we're off to join the world. Curtis, know of any nice tasty dog on to which we can glom?

Florence the Flea

🐾 🐾 🐾

Dear Florence,

Go back to the circus, you bloodsucker!!! And, stay away from my buddies and me!!!

Any dog that has ever had fleas can tell you about the misery you tiny parasites cause. Your saliva is considered one of the more irritating substances on Earth, which is easy to believe when we're frantically scratching ourselves raw all night long. So, Florence, still think I might want to recommend one of my kind for you to glom on? Don't think so.

The good news is that we have relatively new weapons that will either kill adult fleas or sterilize female fleas like yourself so you can no longer lay eggs. Sure, you may give us a few itchy hours but we'll send you and your heirs to your maker! So, back to the circus or, change your name to Ctenocephalides felis and go mess up a few cats...but not if they're living with dogs!!!

  Curtis the Dog

FLORENCE THE FLEA

- **An adult female. She survives by feeding on blood.**
- **Small, wingless and a little larger than a pinhead, she moves fast and can leap great distances (a reason why she's a great circus performer!).**
- **She can occur year-round in warm climates or on pets that live indoors. In colder climates, she'll usually be seen only in warm weather.**
- **Symptoms of her bite include scratching, biting, broken skin and hair loss; bites can also cause a serious skin condition known as FAD (flea allergy dermatitis).**
- **She could carry tapeworms, a harmful intestinal parasite, and heavy infestations can cause anemia and death.**

"If you lie down with dogs, you get up with fleas." - Proverb

ON THE DOG? THEY'RE IN THE HOUSE!

Their favorite meal is dog but they don't necessarily live where they eat, so if the dog has fleas, odds are, so does the home! Carpeting, upholstered furniture, drapes... almost anywhere. When hungry, they'll jump to the nearest animal and even bite humans when looking for a host!

"The fatter the flea the leaner the dog."
- German Proverb

I KNOW YOU'RE THERE , SOMEWHERE!

- Adult fleas, flea dirt, or flea eggs can most easily be seen on a dog's rump and thinly-haired belly.
  - Adult fleas: brown-colored moving spots
  - Flea dirt: Flea feces from digested blood that looks black will appear red-brown when smeared on white paper
  - Flea eggs: Tiny, white sand grains
- The adult fleas one sees represent only 1% of the flea population; the other 99% are mostly unseen eggs and immature developing fleas living in rugs, furniture, pet bedding or outside.

WEAPONS OF FLEA DESTRUCTION (WFD)

- New products such as Program, Frontline and Advantage are available to help rid dogs of fleas.
    - Program, must be ingested, while Frontline and Advantage are topical applications.
- The "collar." Tends to work for at least the first days. However, some say that most collars lose potency over time, and faster if the dog gets wet.
- Some swear that Brewer's Yeast, Garlic, or Vitamin B are effective though there is little scientific evidence to support those remedies.
- Insecticide shampoos from a vet, pet store or supermarket, along with sprays and powders, ointments and baths all claim to be flea preventions. Most of these work but dogs should really be treated either daily or weekly to stop a re-infestation.
- And, as a dog is being treated, so should the home!

Dear Curtis,

As long as they are in the house, Mom and Dad let us hang out pretty much wherever we want. Okay, not on the furniture but anywhere under, around or near it! But, whenever other people come over and good munchies are put on the coffee table, suddenly it's "OUT!" and we're banished to the edges of the room, off the rug and away from all the nice guests who have obviously come over just to pet and admire us! We're feeling so left out. Curtis, what's a party animal to do?

Duster and Jazzie in Edwards, CO

(Note: Duster and Jazzie can be found on page 71)

Dear D & J,

Guests and munchies are two of the things that we canines love the most and when our parents have company over and munchies on the table, we're talking major temptation. Munchies alone are quite seductive for any dog worth its weight in drool and when you add guests to the equation, the potential for "dogs gone wild" is enormous. Just the thought of the "3-C's," cheese, crackers and company, is enough to get me salivating big time!

Usually, in situations like these, most of our parents expect us to behave like good dogs and leave the guests and munchies alone. As you correctly note, the problem is that good dogs are party animals and we crave the action. "Banishing" us to a party's periphery is contrary to our natural behavior and it's not uncommon for us to feel neglected and stressed-out.

So what should you do? Well, you can express your feelings in a number of destructive ways, which hopefully you've learned will only make matters worse. Therefore, ixnay on relieving yourselves on the floor, ripping up clothing or paper goods and chewing on furniture.

Perhaps, a change in your perspective is in order. I mean, think about it, which of these two choices would you prefer? One, to be "banished" when there's company over and munchies on the coffee table or two, crated when there's company over and munchies on the table? And, which of these two choices would you prefer? One, to have the freedom to hang out just about anywhere you'd like in the house when your parents are home or two, not have that freedom?

Personally, I'd choose freedom and I'd rather be banished than crated, especially when the banishment is only temporary. After all, I've found that when there's a party going on in my house, my master is usually so busy with his guests that he hasn't the time to notice me sneaking a munchie or two and there's always at least one guest wanting to be my accomplice! So, my advice? Be patient, be opportunistic and work the room as best as you can! And be a team! There ARE two of you, aren't there?

Curtis the Dog

Dear Curtis,

Every evening for the past several years my masters get home from work and take me to the local dog park. The problem is that at this time of year it gets dark about 4 p.m. and the park has no lighting. The town had initially agreed to put in lighting, which would only be on until 8 p.m., but then several residents living near the park objected. My buddies and me don't understand why the uproar given that there's a horse arena next to the park that has lights on sometimes up to 11 p.m. Curtis, what can we do? It's gotten so bad that some of us are wearing miner's hats.

Poop Park Pooches

Picture by Spencer T. Tucker, NYC Dept. of Parks and Recreation

Dear Pooches,

Evidently those living near the park want to keep it safe for thieves, muggers and other bad people by not lighting it. Or, perhaps, they think horses are man's best friend. Imagine, lights on for horses that wear blinders! I mean, let's see a horse catch a Frisbee or fetch a stick!

Guess those protesting lighting the park must not like dogs. Oh, the irony of their living near a dog park. So here's a suggestion to you and your buddies...instead of pooping in the park where it's so dark that you might step in it yourselves, take your business to the front of their houses. Maybe then they'll see the light.

Curtis the Dog

🐾 🐾 🐾

"Like dogs, bicycles are catalysts that attract a superior category of people." - Chip Brown

🐾 🐾 🐾

"Some days you're the dog, some days you're the hydrant." - Unknown

🐾 🐾 🐾

*"A dog's smile and God's processes
are not understood by anyone."
- Oromos of Ethiopia*

Emmet on the left, Gibson on the right!! (Page 6)

Chloe, longing for poop rolling (Page 22)

Elder Speedster "Cinder" (Page 14)

Donut-eating Nicki (Page 30)

*Bachelor-Pad Murray
(Page 34)*

*Not-the-Car Phoebe
(Page 36)*

Emmett on Poopsicle Alert! (Page 40)

Coco & Her Dancing Partner (Page 42)

Dirty Dancing!!!

An Unhissing Ellie Mae (Page 54)

Duster & Jazzie romping in Edwards, CO
(Pages 62 & 104)

Lilly Feeling Secure With Maggie (Page 100)

An Awake Molly (Page 114)

Barkey Baking Tasty Treats! (Page 98)

Gibson & His Binky! (Page 88)

🐾 🐾 🐾

"The world was conquered through the understanding of dogs; the world exists through the understanding of dogs." - Friedrich Nietzsche

🐾 🐾 🐾

Dear Curtis,

I am a deeply religious person, devotedly attending services and following the traditions and rituals of my faith. Curtis, I know that my dog Crispian begs and wonder whether he prays. Are dogs religious?

Devout Dave in Dover

🐾 🐾 🐾

🐾 🐾 🐾

"A dog is very religious and its religion is free from superstition. The god it believes in is its master, and that god actually exists, and is actually concerned about its welfare, and actually rewards it and punishes it, on a plan comprehensible to dogs and meeting with their approval, for its virtues and vices. Dogs need not waste any time over insoluble theological problems. Their god is plainly visible and wholly understandable - they have no need of clergy to guess for them, mislead them and get them into trouble." - H.L. Mencken, Virgo

🐾 🐾 🐾

Dear Triple D,

There was a time when dogs were thought to be gods or associates of gods. In Egyptian, Greek, Roman, Norse and Hindu mythology, references to dogs are readily found, often in connection with the afterlife or underworld (though we're seen as representing faithful love when we appear with babes like Aphrodite or Venus),

But, that was a long time ago and we now find ourselves prayerful rather than being worshipped. And, according to some scuttle-rump, there are human churches offering us communion and a Jewish synagogue that has a prayer to shield us from fleas! Speaking for myself, I'd rather be medicated or collared...and I prefer a rabbit to a rabbi.

Personally, I don't follow any human religion and I believe that most dogs would bark the same thing. Some of us believe in the great dog god Canus, while others follow a number of wolf-deity sects. Others, still, are non-believers in any deity or religion.

However, whether we believe in a deity or not, we do pray but not for the things people do. We pray for basics like love and food...attention and food...to be played with and food...to be walked or let out and food. Never could understand humans praying for materialistic things or a passing grade on a test or to win a sporting event. In fact, I'm fairly certain that Canus doesn't smile on any one Iditarod team more than another!

Curtis the Dog

"Did you hear about the dyslexic agnostic insomniac who stays up all night wondering if there really is a Dog?" - Unknown

"I wonder if other dogs think poodles are members of a weird religious cult." - Rita Rudner

WELCOME, PILGRIM!!!
Some traditional clergy are welcoming dogs into their flock by offering pet-friendly services, making house calls for sick pets and officiating at pet funerals as a means of dealing with hard-to-fill pews.

"Man is a dog's idea of what God should be."
- Holbrook Jackson

"I care not for a man's religion whose dog and cat are not the better for it." - Abraham Lincoln

LET MY MUMMY GO!

One of the more familiar dogs of myth is Anubis, an ancient Egyptian god that was associated with embalming and mummifaction, and who guided and protected the spirits of the dead as the guardian of both the mummy and the necropolis. Some think that Anubis has the head of a jackal while others say it's a dog. Either way, they're related!

Anubis, ancient Egyptian dog deity looking for his mummy!!!

Dear Curtis,

I live in Seattle, Washington, home to the world-famous Space Needle, the original Starbucks and about more than three feet of rain a year. While it doesn't rain all the time, it rains a lot, sometimes quite heavily, and the skies tend to remain overcast much of the time. When the sky is particularly dark and a heavy rain is predicted, my grandfather often says that "it's time to get out the nets because it's gonna be raining cats and dogs!"

Although I'm only nine years of age, I've seen a lot. But, I've never seen it rain cats and dogs no matter how many times my grandfather says it's going to happen. Curtis, what gives? I really would like a free puppy and I don't care if it's wet but I'm getting tired of standing out in the rain with a net in my hand!

Seattle Sue

🐾 🐾 🐾

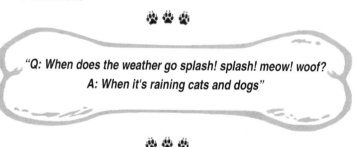

"Q: When does the weather go splash! splash! meow! woof?
A: When it's raining cats and dogs"

🐾 🐾 🐾

Dear Sue,

I'm sorry to bark that you're not going to find a free puppy by standing out in the rain with a net, unless some homeless pooch comes by looking for a place to dry off!

"Raining cats and dogs" is a phrase used to describe weather conditions when there's heavy rain with wind. While there are a number of theories on how this saying came to be, the reality

is that neither dogs nor cats fall from the sky — unless we're caught up in a twister.

So, if your heart's still set on a pupster, I'd suggest you grab your grandfather and visit any one of a number of animal shelters or dog-rescue organizations in the Seattle area. My humans found a wonderful dog at a shelter a few years back — me!

Curtis the Dog

WHAT'S IT MEAN?

The cat symbolizes the down-pouring of rain and the dog the strong gusts of wind that accompany a rainstorm.

- In Northern mythology the cat is supposed to have great influence on the weather.
- English sailors still say that a cat has a "gale of wind" in her tail when she is unusually frisky.
- Witches that rode upon storms were said to assume the form of cats.
- In the Harz Mountains, Germany's most northern mountain range, a stormy northwest wind is called the cat's nose.
- The dog is a signal of wind, like the wolf. Both animals were attendants of Odin, the Norse storm-god.
- In old German pictures, the wind is figured as the "head of a dog or wolf" from which blasts issue.

> "What is worse than raining cats and dogs?
> Hailing taxi cabs!"

HOW ARE THESE FOR REASONS?

- From an unspecified Greek aphorism, "cata doxas", that is similar in sound and which meant "an unlikely occurrence".
- A corrupted version of catadoupe or catdupe, a rare French word meaning a waterfall.
- That during heavy rains in 17th century England, some city streets became raging rivers of filth carrying many cats and dogs, and that people seeing the bodies of drowned dogs and cats floating by thought that they had fallen from the sky.

> "A man came into the house dripping wet and disheveled.
> His sympathetic wife exclaimed, 'Oh, dear. It's raining
> cats and dogs outside!' 'You're telling me,' the man replied.
> 'I just stepped in a poodle'."

"I know Sir John will go, though he was sure it would rain cats and dogs." - Jonathan Swift, A Complete Collection of Polite and Ingenious Conversation, 1738

"When should a mouse carry an umbrella? When it's raining cats and dogs!"

TWO POSSIBILITIES FROM ANIMALPLANET.COM
- The racket made by a storm is similar to the thunderous noise made by fighting cats and dogs.
- When roofs were thatched, downpours would bring cats and dogs that were dozing atop houses down onto the occupants.

"It shall raine...Dogs and Polecats."
- Richard Brome, The City Wit, 1652 (or 3)

Dear Curtis,

Skipper, our 18-month-old Golden Retriever, has earned the unofficial nickname "Psychodog" because he can't stay focused on anything. He runs around like a wild dog, jumping all over us with enthusiasm, chewing on the television remote control, and just can't seem to settle down despite thousands of dollars worth of professional training. Curtis, will he "mature," or are we destined to live with this for years to come?

Lover of ADHD Dog

🐾 🐾 🐾

"Did you ever walk into a room and forget why? I think that is how dogs spend their lives." - Sue Murphy

🐾 🐾 🐾

"You do not own a dog, the dog owns you." - Anonymous

🐾 🐾 🐾

Dear ADHD Dog Lover,

Whether Skipper will outgrow his "wildness" will depend on how you deal with him whether or not he has ADHD.

Generally, young adult dogs can be very active and when you factor in size and a lack of obedience skills, you may find yourself living with a canine-cyclone and wonder whether your dog suffers from some doggy-version of attention-deficit-hyperactivity disorder (ADHD).

As with humans, it can be hard to tell the difference between an ADHD dog and one who is simply "immaturely active," so you should consult with your vet who can administer a test trial to find out. And, should Skipper have ADHD, there are a number of medications and herbal remedies that may help curb Skipper's skipping.

But, let's assume that Skipper is simply an over-active pupster, whose behavior might be due to a number of factors including that he's a Golden Retriever, a high-activity-level breed. When Goldens are doing the work for which they were originally bred, their boundless energy is a positive characteristic but, when they are acquired strictly as pets and companions, without being given the opportunity to do instinctual things, problems can arise.

So, make sure he gets his exercise and we're not just talking about walking-the-dog. If you jog, take Skipper and if you bike, take him, too, as it might be a way to turn Psychodog into Cycledog!

The bottom line is that Skipper is an 18-month old Golden who, despite his size, is still a puppy at heart. Love and patience combined with firmness and consistency over time may be Skipper's miracle drug of choice. I know it's mine!

Curtis the Dog

🐾 🐾 🐾

"If it wasn't for dogs, some people would never go for a walk." - Anonymous

🐾 🐾 🐾

"If your dog is fat, you aren't getting enough exercise." - Unknown

🐾 🐾 🐾

DO I HAVE AN ADHD DOG?

One way to tell is by having your vet run a test trial with a stimulant medication. A normal dog will either show no response or an increase in activity level while biologically hyperkinetic dogs will actually slow down.

Frisco as Cycledog!!!

WHAT CAN CONTRIBUTE TO HYPERACTIVITY?

- The wrong diet, i.e., food containing artificial coloring and/or flavoring.
- A lack of exercise.
- Environmental factors such as children playing and running around the dog or construction workers coming and going from your property, etc.
- A breed's self-preservation and survival instincts.

"When a dog runs at you, whistle for him."
- Henry David Thoreau

TAMING THE WILD DOG!

- Obedience training sessions that are low key, emphasize the "stay" command, have exercises of short duration and involve verbal rather than physical praise have been successful.

- Since dogs are denning animals, confinement to a crate or portable kennel can provide them with a measure of security as well as a 'time-out' period from which both they and their owners could benefit.

- Avoid preservatives, food coloring (those Technicolor dog treats), overly high protein and, of course, sugar.

- No scolding and punishing! This does NOT work for Goldens and it can make them even harder to train!

- Daily exercise. For Goldens, and others like them, brisk walks for a total of 45 minutes a day are just the ticket as well as ball and Frisbee playing, fetch and 'find-it' games, etc.

Dear Curtis,

About a year or so ago, my mom and dad gave birth to a son who looked more like them than do I. Jack's his name (at least that's what they call him, in addition to "baby boy" and "handsome-something or other"...you know, names they used to call me).

Well, Jack now owns millions of colorful, squeaky, shiny and furry TOYS!!!!!!!!!! And I LOVE to eat each and every one of them. I'm quite partial to the plastic ones called "binkies" as they cut down on plaque and give my gums a good workout. Problem is that my mom and dad yell at me for this.

I can understand their point a little bit but I'm mostly mad at these manufacturers who make dog toys and baby toys look, feel and taste the SAME! If these humans really wanted me to give up the block eating, then why do they buy me a plastic ball and then buy him one that looks just like it? I'm tempted to snack everyday...and hence, I get yelled at daily. Curtis, please advise.

Frustrated,

Gibson, a Golden with a Toys R Us "all-you-can eat-card"

P.S. I've tried to explain to mom that the giraffe with one missing ear just teaches "baby boy" about tolerance and acceptance of those with disabilities but, she's not buying it.

(Note: Gibson can be found on page 74)

> *"We've begun to long for the pitter-patter of little feet – so we bought a dog. Well, it's cheaper, and you get more feet." - Rita Rudner*

Dear Gibson,

Sounds like you have a number of issues.

One issue concerns your being jealous of Jack given that you make note of his looking more like "mom and dad" than do you and his being called names that once were reserved for you. Of course, it may just be that Jack's presence has deprived you of some of the attention and affection you got prior to his arrival. Since doing anything to Jack would be akin to drawing a "go-directly-to-the-pound card," my advice here would be for you to...GET OVER IT!

A second issue concerns your love for plastic, which makes me wonder whether your favorite movie is "The Graduate." One reason why dogs eat non-food items has to do with clean and healthy teeth and gums so you may have a good case for gnawing on plastic just as long as it's not one of your parents' credit cards.

A third issue you raise concerns being yelled at. Ouch! Verbal scolding is usually not effective for a number of reasons including different time-realities. Since 1 human-second is about 5-7 dog-seconds we rarely know when it was that we did whatever it was for which they're yelling at us! "Huh, I did what, when?"

A fourth issue has to do with how similar our toys and the toys for human babies are. Oftentimes would-be parents with a dog provide us with toys that resemble baby toys and when baby arrives with its complement of toys, it's easy for us to get confused and think we can play with those too! Obviously, the best solution would have been for your folks to have provided you with toys that did not resemble baby toys but that's putting the rabbit behind the greyhounds. Perhaps, you can talk them into getting you things like

Kong Chew Toys, Hercules Bones and/or Nylabones.

Your fascination with binkies is not surprising as nothing quite compares to a binky from a taste and rubbery texture perspective. Why, even adult humans have a tendency to chew on one! However, your binky-chewing days may be over shortly as Jack becomes a toddler and his toys less resemble yours – unless, of course, Jack has some younger siblings on the way!

Gibson, I know it's not going to be easy but try to keep your nose and mouth out of Jack's toy chest and have your folks keep Jack's toys off the floor. After all, anything and everything on the floor is ours, including the binkies!

Curtis the Dog

WHAT'S WITH THE VARIED DIET?
Eating non-food items like plastic is considered a compulsion called PICA. Some causes have to do with not getting enough food or having to compete for food as a very young pup, while others have to do with not getting enough attention or being bored or anxious. Still other reasons have to do with keeping a dog's teeth and gums clean and healthy.

> *"The dog's kennel is not the place to keep a sausage."* - Danish Proverb

YOU YELLING AT ME?

Interactive punishment, i.e., punishment that comes directly from humans, such as verbal scolding, is usually not effective because dogs might interpret it as attention – much as some human children have negative behavior for attention-getting purposes.

Further, punishment after the fact is rarely helpful since dogs don't understand that they're being punished for something they may have done hours, minutes or even seconds before.

> *"A dog teaches a boy fidelity, perseverance, and to turn around three times before lying down."*
> *- Robert Benchley*

> *"What are little boys made of?*
> *Frogs and snails, And puppy dog tails.*
> *That's what little boys are made of."* - Unknown

Dear Curtis,

I just "inherited" an older dog from Emma, my late next door-neighbor. She was an elderly lady whom I only knew from seeing in the hallway, from exchanging greetings and from petting Harry.

A month ago Emma became ill, and early last week she passed away. None of her relatives wanted Harry and, after hearing of their plans to dispose of him, I offered to take the dog. Long story short, I've never had a dog before and I don't know the slightest thing about caring for one, much less an older one. Curtis, what guidance can you provide on caring for Harry?

Good Neighbor Pam

Dear Good Neighbor,

What a wonderful human you are to take Harry into your home and life, especially since you've never had one of us live with you before and the fact that he's a senior.

Like people, dogs are individual in the way we age and, like people, we're living longer thanks to caring and knowledgeable humans who provide us with a healthy diet, adequate exercise, proper and timely veterinary care, a clean environment and, of course, LOVE...lots and lots of love!

Your greatest ally in keeping your dog happy and healthy while promoting long-life will be your veterinarian. Since Harry is your first dog and given that you did not indicate living with another animal, I'd suggest asking those you know with pets for recommendations. Then, check them out and if you don't like what you see or hear or feel, move on and continue your search.

Pam, Harry is a lucky dog. Not only was he spared whatever outcome Emma's relatives may have planned for him, but he also found you. The great dog god Canus certainly must have been smiling on him...and on you. There's a reason why your path and Harry's crossed and there's a reason why the two of you are now together. Whatever it is will reveal itself in due time though one thing is presently evident...you're more than a good neighbor; you're a good person with a heart of kibble!

Curtis the Dog

PS. I've included some advice on caring for an older dog and on finding a vet on pages 96 & 97!

LIVING & LICKING LONGER
The average lifespan for dogs has increased from 7 years in the 1930's to more than 12 years today and, with the right care, it's not uncommon for dogs to live to the ripe old age of 14 or 15!

"You're only a dog old fellow, a dog and you've had your day; But never a friend of all my friends has been truer than you always." - Julian Stearns Cutler

HOW OLD IS IT?

The point at which a dog qualifies as 'aged' varies. Veterinarians generally consider small dogs to be senior citizens at about 12 years of age, while large dogs reach the senior stage at 6 to 8 years of age, which roughly corresponds to the 55-plus category in people.

Tufts University published the following guidelines to define a senior dog:

Age in Dog Yrs.	A Dog's Age in Human Years			
	Up to 20 lbs.	21-50 lbs.	51-90 lbs	Over 90 lbs.
5	36	37	40	42
6	40	42	45	49
7	44	47	50	56
8	48	51	55	64
9	52	56	61	71
10	56	60	66	78
11	60	65	72	86
12	64	69	77	93
13	68	74	82	101
14	72	78	88	108
15	76	83	93	115
16	80	87	99	123
17	84	92	104	
18	88	96	109	
19	92	101	115	
20	96	105	120	

Chart developed by Dr. Fred L. Metzger, DVM, State College, PA. Courtesy of Pfizer Animal Health.

OTHER FACTORS INFLUENCING A DOG'S AGING
Aside from age and weight, factors that influence an older dog's aging process, and the corresponding age-related problems it may eventually have, are:

- **Genetic Background** -- Some breeds are known to have specific health problems.
- **Nutrition** -- Good nutrition will retard the aging process so watch his weight!
- **Illnesses & Disease** -- A serious illness or disease can shorten a dog's life.
- **Control of Environmental Factors** -- Keeping your dog and his environment clean and free of parasites will increase the chances of long life.

KEEPING AN OLDER DOG HEALTHY

The Senior Dogs Project, http://www.srdogs.com, considers these the ten most important tips to keep an older dog healthy:

1. Establish a relationship with a veterinarian you trust and with whom you feel comfortable.

2. Be informed on conditions common to older dogs and be alert to their symptoms, promptly bringing them to your vet's attention when they occur.

3. Feed your oldster the best food you can afford and consider two small meals daily rather than a large one.

4. Don't overfeed as obesity can shorten its life.

5. Consider the use of dietary supplements.

6. Give adequate exercise based on your dog's condition.

7. Regularly brush your dog's teeth and have them professionally cleaned when advised.

8. Have your dog vaccinated once every three years.

9. Control fleas and ticks, and keep your dog and his environment clean.

10. Make your dog as much a part of your life as possible, and do all you can to keep him interested, active, happy and comfortable.

> *"Blessed is the person who has earned the love of an old dog."* - Sydney Jeanne Seward

FINDING A VET/ANIMAL HOSPITAL

Ask those you know with pets for recommendations. Then, make an appointment and check them out!

How clean is the facility? Is it well-lit? Does it have laboratory equipment? Is there gas anesthesia? Is it accredited by the American Animal Hospital Association (AAHA), a sign of high veterinary care standards? Are the office hours and payment policy convenient? Don't forget to get a hospital brochure or welcome letter that explains hospital policies and procedures.

And, meet the vet! Is he/she able to communicate with you? Does he/she make it comfortable to ask questions?

Even if the doctor is highly qualified or the facility highly recommended, if what you see, hear or feel isn't quite right, you may need to go elsewhere.

Dear Curtis,

I'm a 20-something first-time mother of a 3-month old baby girl. Prior to her birth, I was a full-time paralegal planning on finishing my education and getting my law degree.

Now, all I want to do is stay home with Alice and, of course, Barney, my 5-year old Keeshond. Well, that's not entirely true as I do get very bored at times and feel a need to be productive. I've gotten together with a number of women who are in a similar situation and we're looking into starting a home-based business. Among the things we're investigating is a gourmet dog bakery and have heard of many such businesses around the country. Curtis, are these bakeries something for real or just a fad?

Biscuit Baking Betty

(Note: Picture of Barkey the Baker on page 73)

Dear BBB,

Gourmet dog bakeries are no fad, but are born out of humans' desire for a more healthy life and diet for both themselves and their pooches. Wishing to avoid negative effects associated with chemical preservatives in commercial dog food, a huge demand for natural treats grew, causing the gourmet dog bakery market to take off despite the relatively high price associated with their products.

But, it's not just about being healthy as these treats also taste great, and among some of the wholesome, "good-for-canine" treats are custom cakes and cookies (complete with a picture of a dog's breed), as well as doggie pizzas, truffles, cannoli, biscotti and cupcakes. Yum!!!

While nowadays you can find a gourmet dog bakery in most

upscale areas around the country and, most certainly, on the Internet where delicious treats and snacks for yours truly can be ordered, there should still be opportunities.

So, Betty, why don't you and your friends seriously look into starting your own highly profitable home-based "barkery." Books on how to start such a business, as well as recipes, can be found in bookstores or online and I strongly recommend that you contact some of the gourmet dog bakeries that are on the web for information and insight.

Please let me know how you are progressing with this venture and, by all means, send me some samples!!! Double Yum!!!

Curtis the Dog

LOTS OF MONEY IN PETS!
In 1998, Forbes magazine reported that dog owners spent $9 billion a year on pet food, compared with $6 billion for baby food!

ALL NATURAL AND YUMMY!
Gourmet treats are baked without chemical preservatives, salt or sugar and made with high quality, human-grade natural ingredients that include whole grains, peanut butter, apples, tomatoes, carob, garlic, yogurt, cream cheese, honey and oats.

Dear Curtis,

My name is Lilly and I'm an adorable 3-year old calico cat. I've been living with my family for a little over 2 years, one that I picked out after my former owner left me in the woods one Fall day to fend for myself. As I live in Maine, it was critical for me to find a home before cold weather set in.

Scouting a neighborhood, I came upon a house that had a very pretty red dog, some sort of hound, that I distantly watched for a couple of days. She seemed fun-loving, happy and well-treated and I figured this was important if I was going to live there. So, after a few more days, and with me getting colder and lonelier, I made my move and there I was, in the house.

After I moved in, I tested things out a little bit with Maggie — that's the hound's name — by rubbing up against her legs. She didn't seem to mind and, so, a little while later, I started lying down next to her. It felt soooo good to snuggle with a furry friend again as I really missed my mom and siblings. I figured Maggie was a good substitute so, eventually, I started to groom her, licking her ears and neck. She's never stopped me but she's never sought me out or nuzzled me either. Oh yeah, once in a while she'll sniff my head (or my butt) but she just doesn't seem to show any affection.

Also, Maggie loves to play and wrestle with our master but she just won't play with me. I try running after her and stand on top of the couch as she goes by, reaching out for her, but she just doesn't respond. I do sometimes play with her tail while she is wrestling with "dad" and she just gives me a dirty look.

So, Curtis, how can I get her to interact more with me? All I want is for her to play with me a little bit. I really have grown to love her and think of her as my big sister. I think she likes me, but I'm awfully frustrated. Sure I know she is older than me, she's about 9, but she acts like a puppy when she plays with Dad. So, why won't she play with me? I'm not asking for much, am I?

Sincerely,

Lilly

(Note: Lilly and Maggie can be found on page 72)

🐾 🐾 🐾

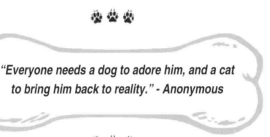

"Everyone needs a dog to adore him, and a cat to bring him back to reality." - Anonymous

🐾 🐾 🐾

Dear Lilly,

I wish I could give you better news. I wish I could tell you that one day all your dreams as they relate to Maggie will be fulfilled. I wish I could tell you that Maggie's feelings for you will turn from an indifferent coexistence to the playful, close, warm and intimate relationship you seek. Alas, I fear it may not come to be.

While there are tales and tails of love between a canine and feline, far too many of them are nothing but romantic fantasies like the films that come out of Doggywood.

To begin with, you and Maggie are two different species with two different personas and agendas. Secondly, there is that age difference. It's not about Maggie being about nine and you being a little under three. The reality is that you're in your late twenties and

Maggie is in her early fifties. So, there's about a 25-year age difference between the two of you, which makes her old enough to be your mother! And, having lived with people, I've seem some human mothers just tolerate their daughters – no more, no less — and, sadly for you, that may be Maggie's attitude as well.

Sure, she lets you snuggle up next to her and groom her but, as you said yourself, she doesn't reciprocate with the kind of love and affection that you would like. GET OVER IT! And, be grateful for the tolerance and affection that she does show you. After all, it's not like she has you in fear or terror, is it?

As far as Maggie playing with Dad and not playing with you that way...you're not Dad and her relationship with him is not comparable to her relationship with you.

Lilly, my advice is for you to be thankful for the wonderful life you now have and to think about it relative to where you were...in the woods with winter closing in...and not relative to your not feeling love or being played with as much as you would like. You're not being ignored, are you? So, stop being an insecure cat and take comfort in the fact that Maggie hasn't bitten your silly feline head off.

Curtis the Dog

"A dog is like a liberal. He wants to please everybody. A cat really doesn't need to know that everybody loves him." - William Kunstler

LET'S COMPARE AGES!!!

The "old" belief that both a dog's and cat's lives relative to that of a human was 1 year dog/cat to every 7 years human is no longer true.   The 1-to-7 ratio only exists for a year or two and then the difference between number of animal years to a human year is about 5 years.

"If a dog jumps in your lap, it is because he is fond of you, but if a cat does the same thing, it is because your lap is warmer." - Alfred North Whitehead

Dear Curtis,

    With all the good stuff that can be found to eat up here in the mountains (sticks, rocks, deer & bear poop, etc.), we sometimes get upset stomachs. Why do Mom and Dad freak out when we give it back on that nice soft custom-designed Indian rug in the living room? Do they really expect us to hurl on the hard stone floor, the slippery wood parts or that cheesy nylon wall-to-wall when we're feeling rotten and need all the comfort we can get? We're confused. Curtis, can you please explain this mean attitude on their part?

        Duster and Jazzie again, in Edwards CO

        (Note: Duster & Jazzie can be found on page 71)

Dear D & J, again!

    Sticks and rocks and poop? Oh my!

    Humans with dogs have to expect that we're going to have an upset stomach every now and then, especially when you consider the exotic nature of some of the things we wolf down! And, they have to realize that we're not the kind that will wake them up in the middle of the night, say something like "Mommy, my tummy hurts," and then puke our brains out on them, their pajamas, sheets, blankets and pillows.

    Besides, and while I can't speak for your folks, I believe there's no way most humans are going to be sticking out their hands and trying to catch our upchuck on the way to the bathroom!

    So, we seek comfort in other places. The fact that you seem to prefer a nice soft custom-designed Indian rug is simply a reflection of your appreciation for some of the finer things in life. And I'm with you as far as hard stone, slippery wood and cheesy nylon is concerned. I mean, who decorated that house? A cat?

By the way, the reason your parents freak out has nothing to do with you. It has to do with the way their human parents raised them and I can recommend a therapist if they'd like. So, recognize this and use it to your advantage.

The next time you're not feeling well and need to hurl, find a place that will freak them out more than the Indian rug and do it there. And do it there the next one or two times you need to "lose your Milk bones." After a while, they might not mind it so much if you went back to the rug! Meanwhile, gotta run and find some grass. Seems something I ate is not agreeing with me!

Curtis the Dog

Vomit Mold. Yuck!!!

Dear Curtis,

We were inspired to write to you after reading the letter that Florence the Flea wrote. A flea! What a joke! You were absolutely right in telling her to pack up and take her family back to the circus. That way they can leave more of the juicy red stuff to us! We're ticks and unlike those pesky fleas, we do get under your skin, and we can cause some real nasty stuff for you and humans. Ever hear of Lyme disease? How about Rocky Mountain Spotted Fever? Paralysis, anyone? Anyhow, Curtis, it's getting warm again and I just wanted to let you know that we'll be looking for you!!!

Timmy the Tick and Friends

Dear Timmy and Friends,

You guys really tick my kind and me off. You not only ruin our enjoyment of the outdoors but also that of humans, cats and other mammals. And, you carry a number of infectious organisms that can transmit diseases. Why, it's as if we need armor when we're romping in the woods, playing in the yard, hiking, camping and picnicking with our humans or simply relieving ourselves. And, it's not as if there are lots of places to go to avoid you as your habitats are varied and extensive.

The good news is that there are virtually hundreds of approved or licensed pesticides and repellents to control ticks on us or our environment and our vet should be consulted to determine which one is best for our individual needs.

Even so, a daily check of us during tick season is still essen-

tial and should any be found on us, they're to be removed with a sterilized tweezers — so ixnay on the match, mineral oil, nail polish or petroleum jelly.

So, Timmy, threatening my kind and me? Well, go ahead. There's just so much we can do to totally prevent bloodsuckers like you from getting to us. However, we have a Lyme disease vaccine at our disposal and antibiotics have been effective in treating tick-borne diseases that infect us.

Bottom line is that we're not going to let your presence prevent us from enjoying the great outdoors. After all, it belongs to us and you're just a pest whose days are numbered.

Curtis the Dog

TIMMY THE TICK & FRIENDS
- **Over 200 varieties of ticks in the U.S.**
- **They're arachnids like mites, spiders and scorpions and not insects like fleas.**
- **Habitats include woods, beach grass, lawns, forests and even urban areas.**
- **Season generally occurs during the summer months but a warm spring can activate them in April.**
- **Carriers of various infectious organisms that can transmit diseases to dogs and other mammals.**

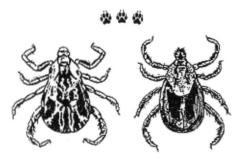

Male (left) and female American dog tick, *Dermacentor variabilis*

TICK-BORNE DISEASES W/POSSIBLE SYMPTOMS
- **Babesiosis: lethargy, appetite loss, weakness, pale gums.**
- **Ehrlichiosis: high fever, muscle aches.**
- **Lyme disease: lameness, swollen joints, fever, poor appetite, fatigue and vomiting (some infected animals show no symptoms). States listed as "endemic" areas for Lyme disease are New York, Massachusetts, Pennsylvania, New Jersey, Connecticut, Rhode Island, Wisconsin, Minnesota and California.**
- **Tick paralysis in dogs: gradual paralysis, seen first as an unsteady gait from uncoordinated back legs (some infected dogs don't develop paralysis).**

> **MAKING THE ENVIRONMENT ANTI-TICK**
> - Keep grass well-clipped and remove brush to reduce humidity around property.
> - Prune trees to allow more sunlight to penetrate to the soil surface.
> - Apply a limited insecticide spray to the edges of lawns, along paths or trails to minimize tick movement into lawns or other areas.

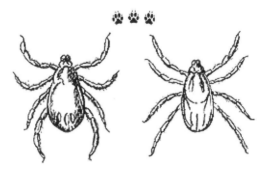

Male (left) and female brown dog tick, *Rhipicephalus sanguineus*

> **FEELING FOR TICKS ON A DOG**
> Rub your hands all over its body, and your fingers through its fur, applying enough pressure to feel any abnormalities in the skin. If you feel a small lump, pull the fur apart for further investigation. An embedded tick will look like a small black or brown pimple, sometimes flat-ish and, sometimes, with its legs visible.

🐾 🐾 🐾

REMOVING A TICK FROM FIDO

Once a tick is found, you're to remove it immediately by going at it with tweezers that have been sterilized with alcohol or over a flame. Then, get the tweezers between the dog's skin and the tick's jaws, and gently pull, with a side-to-side motion if it isn't budging. The main ingredient is patience, and a steady, gentle and firm pull over a few minutes time usually tires out the tick enough to release its grip. The goal is to remove the entire tick so be careful not to yank the tick's body from its head and create a bigger problem. Should this happen, keep the area clean and call your vet for further instructions.

Old methods of burning a tick off or smothering it with mineral oil, petroleum jelly or nail polish are no longer acceptable and ticks should never be squeezed when they're being removed as it might further inject infectious material into the dog.

🐾 🐾 🐾

"The word 'politics' is derived from the word 'poly', meaning 'many', and the word 'ticks' meaning 'blood sucking parasites'." - Larry Haridman

"You think Nature is some Disney movie? Nature is a killer. Nature is a bitch. It's feeding time out there 24 hours a day, every step you take is a gamble with death. If it isn't getting hit with lightning today, it's an earthquake tomorrow or some deer tick carrying Lyme Disease. Either way, you're ending up on the wrong end of the food chain."
- Jeff Melvoin, Northern Exposure, Bolt from the Blue, 1994

Dear Curtis.

It's me again, your pal Cleo. The meow in the alley is that you're pretty smart for a dog, though you're still light years behind us cats.

One of the reasons is because we're smart enough not to work. I mean, why should we? Oh, I guess some humans might think that catching mice is work but it's really entertainment for us. Yep, all we need to do to be fed and housed is be ourselves…aloof, independent, ornery when we feel like it, controlling…you know like royalty or a god.

Why, even the amount of love we receive from humans is up to us! So, Curtis, go ahead and earn your keep while my kind and me find a nice sunbeam in which to sleep. A smart dog? Now there's an oxymoron!

Cleo the Calico

🐾 🐾 🐾

"Dogs are wise. They crawl away into a quiet corner and lick their wounds and do not rejoin the world until they are whole once more." - Agatha Christie

🐾 🐾 🐾

"If skill could be gained by watching, every dog would become a butcher." - Turkish Proverb

🐾 🐾 🐾

Dear Cleo,

So dogs aren't as smart as cats because we choose to work? That just shows how dumb felines are! Yes, we work. Whether we're sheepherders, detectives, household helpers or more, we're doggone good workers! And work makes us happy. We're not salaried but then, we're paid in something a lot more valuable...love!

We serve as eyes for blind humans, ears for deaf ones and as an aide for others with disabilities. In fact, we can open and close doors, switch lights on and off, pick up dropped objects and even pull wheelchairs. And, we bring joy to senior citizens and those who are ill.

We pull sleds, help solve crimes, keep out illegal drugs and food, detect bombs and money, hunt for missing persons, even when covered by an avalanche, and much, much more. And, we worked side-by-flank with rescue workers in New York City after 9/11.

Less smart than cats? Maybe so but the quality of one's life is not measured by intelligence. We help make the world a better place for ourselves and for humans. Remind me, what do cats do?

Curtis the Dog

🐾 🐾 🐾

**"Dogs believe they are human.
Cats believe they are God." - Anonymous**

🐾 🐾 🐾

Dear Curtis,

My dog Molly slept a lot as most dogs do... after all, it's a dog's life and "it's har-r-r-d work" as we all know! Sometimes while she was sleeping her legs would suddenly twitch, she would give a muffled bark and then she would wake herself up, look at me and flap her ears (as if I were the one who had caused all the commotion). Curtis, what could she have been dreaming about to get her so riled up?

Puzzled in Birmingham

(Note: Mollie can be found on page 72)

"Like a dog, he hunts in dreams."
- Alfred Lord Tennyson

Dear Puzzled,

You're correct in thinking that Molly was probably dreaming though some, especially cats, believe we're incapable of it.

While we dream for shorter periods of time than do people, we tend to do so with more action — twitching or moving our legs as if running or digging; chewing, licking or moving our lips and whiskers; whining, whimpering or yipping as if excited; and breathing rapidly or holding our breath for a brief time.

As for what Molly could have been dreaming about, I don't know. Some of my buddies dream about chasing something: a car, a ball, a criminal, a rabbit, or a cat! Some dream about digging for or chomping on a nice juicy bone. And, sometimes it's a nightmare and in it we're running away from something or someone, perhaps an abusive owner or the dogcatcher.

When we're relaxed and dreaming, it's hard for us to be awakened so I'm not surprised that Molly, upon startling herself awake, gave you a "what gives" look . She was probably trying to figure out what happened to the field in which she was just romping.

Personally speaking, I tend to dream about female dogs, dinner parties, car trips in a convertible, having my ears rubbed and belly scratched, being with my human and canine buddies, chasing a cat (or two)...and female dogs! Woof!

   Curtis the Dog

DREAMING, A NECESSITY OF LIFE

As in humans, dreaming in dogs seems to be a necessity in the normal processing of data and storing of memory.   Dogs do think and have memory and, so, need to purge and reorganize their memory banks during sleep just as humans do.

Adult dogs spend about 10-to-12% of their sleeping time in rapid-eye-movement (REM) sleep, the state in which dreams occur.   Pupsters spend a much greater proportion of their sleep time in REM sleep, no doubt compacting huge quantities of newly acquired data.

"People's dreams are made out of what they do all day. The same way a dog that runs after rabbits will dream of rabbits. It's what you do that makes your soul, not the other way around." - Barbara Kingsolver

BOY, DID I HAVE A DREAM!

Like humans, dogs have two main types of sleep: slow wave sleep (SWS), the first stage, in which mental processes are muted but muscle tone remains, and rapid eye movement (REM) sleep, in which the body is fully relaxed but the mind races with eyes darting rapidly. It is in REM sleep when dogs, like humans, dream.

"The human imagination...has great difficulty in living strictly within the confines of a materialist practice or philosophy. It dreams, like a dog in its basket, of hares in the open." - John Berger

"Let sleeping dogs lie."
- American Proverb

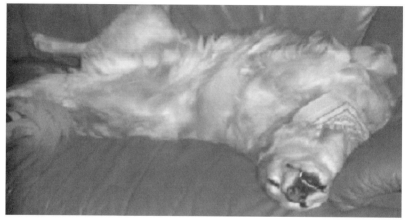

Picture of Curtis, courtesy of Matt Gersten

LET DREAMING DOGS DREAM

Dogs can be difficult to awaken when in REM sleep given that they're so relaxed. So, it's important not to attempt to wake them when they're dreaming unless it is absolutely necessary. If their sounds and motions are disturbing, crinkle a piece of paper or clear your throat in an attempt to change the pattern of the dream without completely waking the dog up.

Dear Curtis,

Two of my buddies down the street from me ingested poison last month while playing in their wrought iron fenced-in-yard. One of them, Sparky, died. As if that's not bad enough, it's being investigated as a possible deliberate animal poisoning. Both dogs were 3-year olds from the same boxer or pit bull-mix mother and neither barked excessively. Authorities are theorizing that the person who did this may have assumed they were aggressive because of their appearance.

Thankfully, I'm a cute little Pomeranian. Even so, Curtis, I'm worried that there may be a serial dog killer around.

Afraid Of The Backyard

🐾 🐾 🐾

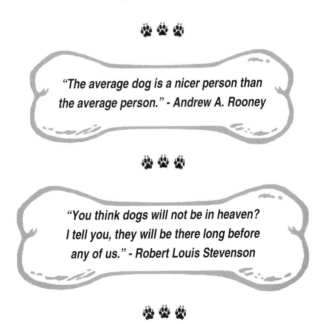

"The average dog is a nicer person than the average person." - Andrew A. Rooney

🐾 🐾 🐾

"You think dogs will not be in heaven? I tell you, they will be there long before any of us." - Robert Louis Stevenson

🐾 🐾 🐾

Dear Afraid,

Truly saddened by the news of your buddies and troubled that they may have been poisoned because they were pit-bull look-alikes. Makes it hard for us canines to be peoples' best friend when there are humans who poison us because of our appearance. Of course we don't know the whole story. Still, it's hard to believe that anything those dogs did, given no report of pillaging or plundering, warranted a death sentence.

Guess I shouldn't be surprised. After all, humans have been persecuting and killing fellow humans because of their appearance since they first appeared on this planet, which, I might add, was after us dogs! Guess I am naïve to hope that humans might learn to play nice by hanging around with us. Shame.

Meanwhile, to my fellow canines, I know it's tough but remember...not everything that smells good is good for us to eat. Let's be careful out there!

Curtis the Dog

🐾 🐾 🐾

🐾 🐾 🐾

Dear Curtis,

I normally wouldn't do this, but I heard you know a lot about bitches. I am a three-year old black & white male kitty who is having trouble with my fat and lazy female feline roommate. She won't leave me alone. Whenever I find a special spot in the house to sleep, she tries to take it from me. She eats all her food and then goes to my dish and eats mine. That's probably why she's so fat. She struts around like she's the only one that lives here. Granted, she was here first, but, it's a big place and there's plenty of room.

I am very busy in my life and I just don't have time for all this. I am presently studying birds out my window, Humming-birds, in particular. I also like to work out and just got some new equipment…"Miss Mousey," "Cozy Cuddles Stair Climber" and an upgraded version of "Chase Your Tail."

I hope all this isn't an indication that she is attracted to me because I want none of it. She's way too old for me -- almost ten and missing most of her teeth. Ugh! Besides, my two-legged mommy took me someplace, and when I woke up I was missing my package. Since then I have completely focused on my career. Birds!

I have attempted to take a swipe at her, but my two-legged mommy made that horrible clapping sound with her paws and yelled "no kitty fighting in this house." I have never hit a woman but, Curtis, I'm afraid that I am at the end of my rope.

Apples the Cat

P.S. I'd like you to know that Cleo the Calico doesn't represent all of our kind. Also heard she wasn't a real Calico.

Dear Apples,

I'm flattered that you would write to me about a relationship between two cats. However, I must counsel you that my response will be from the canine perspective and my instincts toward felines are generally not positive, though I once had a cat roommate named Mouser whom I liked.

With that said, it seems that you're not willing to tolerate, accept and pay your roommate the respect she deserves as the older kitty into whose house you were brought. And, you're also unable or unwilling to step up to the litter box and stake out your territory.

You complain about her not leaving you alone, about her trying to take away favorite spots of yours and eating your food. Well, what are you doing to educate your roommate on your need for privacy? Okay, okay, so you attempted to swipe her and got caught by "mommy." So what? I'm sure there are plenty of occasions when you could express your feelings with a swipe or two when "mommy's" not around, so what's preventing you? And what's with this "mommy" stuff? You're a three-year old cat for barking out loud, which means you're about twenty-eight in human years! Aren't you a little old to be calling your human "mommy"?

Anyhow, back to you and your roommate. You say you enjoy working out and just got some new equipment so it doesn't appear as if you're a weenie. Come now, give her a swipe or two...or a hiss. Show your fangs...get angry...you're a cat for Canus' sake. The King of the Jungle's in your blood! Are you going to let some cross between Garfield and the Witches of Endor get in your way and tell you where to lie, how much you can eat and whether you can leisurely study birds?

As far as her being attracted to you...probably not! If any-thing, she might view you as a younger brother or a son but more likely, just a roommate. Whatever! The bottom line is that you would prefer to be an only cat but the reality is that you're not!

GET OVER IT!!!

Stop complaining and realize that while she's not going to change, you can. You either learn to cohabit with your roommate and show her the respect she deserves being a 10-year old cat (56-years in human terms) who had the house all to herself before you got there or, give her a wide berth. However, if all else fails and she continues to pester and eat your food, assert yourself!!! What are you? A scaredy-cat?

Curtis the Dog

"Cats can be cooperative when something feels good, which, to a cat, is the way everything is supposed to feel as much of the time as possible." - Roger A. Caras

Watcha lookin' at? *A bird, go away!*
Can I have some of your food? *No, go away!*
Wanna lie down near each other? *No. You're fat, lazy and missing teeth. Go away!*

"Nothing's more playful than a young cat, nor more grave than an old one." - Thomas Fuller

"Ignorant people think it's the noise which fighting cats make that is so aggravating, but it ain't so; it's the sickening grammar they use." - Mark Twain

Dear Curtis,

A friend of mine had his dog for 10 years. It was dying from lung cancer and he knew he needed to put the dog down. However, it took my friend a week to gather up the courage to do the right thing even though I kept telling him he had to. Was there something else I should have said or done to have helped him end the dog's suffering sooner than he did?

Also, now that the dog's gone, he is having a tough time because for years, all he did was work and take care of his dog six days a week – and on the seventh day, ride his motorcycle...and take care of his dog. Curtis, what can I do or say to help him?

A Friend Whose Friend Lost His Best Friend

"God will prepare everything for our perfect happiness in heaven, and if it takes my dog being there, I believe he'll be there." - Billy Graham

"The dog is a gentleman; I hope to go to his heaven, not man's." - Mark Twain

Dear Friend,

My sincere condolences to your friend on the passing of his buddy. Dying and death and grieving are not fun, especially when it concerns a loved one whether it be human, canine or, Canus forgive, feline. And the decision to end a life for most humans, whether it be theirs, another human's or a pet's, is never an easy one to make and open to review and second-guessing long after it was made.

That your friend deeply loved his dog is beyond question and so is whether he cared for it. In fact, you make it sound as if a large part of your friend's life revolved around his dog.

Personally, I know that it's extremely hard to let go of someone you deeply love and even harder when you're letting go of that someone by ending their life, even though you know in your heart that it's the right thing. Sometimes, an extra hour or an extra day is all we ask for, as selfish as that may appear.

From where I sit, your friend did what he needed to do as well as what his buddy needed from him. As his friend, you should not judge him as lacking courage, taking longer than he should have or prolonging his dog's suffering. You see, the time it took for him to act was the time that it was going to take, no more and no less.

In view of this, whatever else you could have said or done to expedite the dog's passing wouldn't have mattered. The bottom line is that if your friend still considers you a friend, whatever you did say or do was okay with him, and you should now focus on helping him grieve.

To help him grieve you should recognize that he lost his best friend for the past 10 years. When the dog passed on, he not only lost his pal, his buddy, his roommate, his companion, but, given what you wrote about how your friend spent every day of every week taking care of his dog, he also lost a big part of his own life.

The only thing I can suggest, other than you empathizing and sympathizing with your friend, is to keep reminding him that the dog is in a better place and is no longer suffering from the cancer that took its life.

Again, my sincerest condolences to your friend on the passing of his best friend. I'll go bury a bone in its memory.

Curtis the Dog

"Many years ago when an adored dog died, a great friend, a bishop, said to me, 'You must always remember that, as far as the Bible is concerned, God only threw the humans out of Paradise'." - Unknown

"If there are no dogs in Heaven, then when I die I want to go where they went." - Will Rogers

"If I have any beliefs about immortality, it is that certain dogs I have known will go to heaven, and very, very few persons." - James Thurber

"Heaven goes by favour. If it went by merit, you would stay out and your dog would go in."
- Mark Twain

Headstone at Coon Dog Cemetery, Colbert County, Alabama

Dear Curtis,

I NEED HELP!!!!!!!!!!!!

I'm 15 years old and on my way out...and I really didn't want to leave this world and go to doggie heaven until now. See, I've been living with my mom and dad all my life and up until fifteen months ago, it was just me, my folks and their two daughters, now 7 and 9 years old, whom I truly enjoy, even though they used to put me in dresses and jewels. But now, there's this 15-month old addition and he's terrorizing me.

The other day he snuck into the bathroom, pulled out all of mommy's sanitary pads, removed the sticky part and stuck the pads to my body. I was running around the house (which is a feat in itself nowadays) looking for help until I finally just fell on the floor and went to sleep, covered in panty shields.

Curtis, doesn't this kid know with whom he's messing? I'm a Boxer for goodness sake. My manhood is at stake and I'm too old for this crap. What should I do beside pray for death?

Tyson the Boxer

> *"When a child is locked in the bathroom with water running and he says he's doing nothing but the dog is barking, call 911." - Erma Bombeck*

Dear Tyson,

My sympathy for being with masters who have other things on their minds than the well-being of a trusted friend and family member for the past 15 years. More importantly though, they appear to have more things on their minds than the well-being of their son as they should never leave their toddler-delinquent alone with a dog, even if it's a good-natured, gentle-souled pooch as yourself.

Your parents have to teach their almost toothless terrorist how to properly behave around dogs in general and you in particular – for its own sake. Dogs and kids can be the best or the worst matches. However, there's no reason why you and the child cannot happily coexist if mom and dad are responsible dog owners and parents. The puzzling thing is that there are two older kids suggesting that, at one time, there was harmony in the household between you and a child. Perhaps your folks need a refresher course and, if so, you should drag them to a local bookstore, or to the Internet, where books on raising a child with a dog are available.

Tyson, praying to the god Euthanasia to come and take you away from "Tot-the-Tormentor" is unacceptable. I'm a firm believer in every dog having his day and that every day IS our day! Praying for death to deliver you will only result in increased unhappiness and depression and that's no way to be toward the end of one's life. So, be happy and try to increase the distance between you and the child until it ages a bit and becomes more considerate of its elders, regardless of whether they have two or four legs.

Curtis the Dog

> **TODDLER ALERT!!!**
> Most problems that arise between a dog and child oc-
> cur when the child begins crawling and walking, at
> about a year or so, and parents need to recognize that
> children at that age can be threatening to dogs given
> that they are at eye level, have higher voices, faster
> motions, often forget to use gentle hands and can be
> unpredictable.

"*Dachshunds are ideal dogs for small children, as they are already stretched and pulled to such a length that the child cannot do much harm one way or the other.*" - Robert Benchley

DOG BITES TOT! CLAIMS SELF-DEFENSE!

Pulling ears and tails, running like crazy, teasing, hitting, cornering a dog, tormenting a dog when a dog is sleeping, etc., can lead to a nip or worse.

Though most dogs have learned to tolerate all of their body parts being touched, having food and toys taken from them and various sounds, even the best trained dog has its limits and can bite if hurt or pushed enough. Many dog bites are not directly the fault of the biter and are instigated by a child. On bad days, and at times when a dog may not be feeling well, a pulled ear that normally would be ignored could this time end in a bite.

Dear Curtis,

Something is terribly wrong with me and I can't quite put my paw on it. I haven't been feeling myself, almost as if I'm a cat in dog's clothing except that, as a rule, we don't wear clothes. There was a time when one of my greatest pleasures was riding in a car, moving from side-to-side in the back and occasionally moving from the back to the front and then back again and sticking my head out the window to feel a wonderful rush of air whipping across my face and making my ears fly. Now, I dread going for a car ride and I don't know why. Perhaps it's due to all the stories I'm hearing about bad things that have happened to dogs in cars. Curtis, can you help me?

Slade, Former Shotgun Rider

Dear Slade,

There are lots of reasons why we should be okay about riding in a car. The main one is that there will be times when we need to see our doctor. And, whether it's for a check-up, a shot or something of a more serious nature, it's probably best that a ride in the car doesn't add to any anxiety that we might already have about visiting the vet. However, for a number of us, riding in the car is not a pleasant experience and, contrary to popular human belief, not all of us love trucks and not all of us love cars. In fact, many times when people believe we're chasing after cars, we're really chasing them away!

While movement of the car can make us sick, oftentimes it's due more to the stress of riding in the car and, so, the best way to overcome our fear is for us to be conditioned to recognize the car as a safe place and as a conveyance to wonderful experiences.

A good conditioning program (see page 135) is a step-by-step process that can be applied whether a dog is a novice car rider or a veteran who has become fearful. Done over several weeks, a good program involves us, our human, the car (duh!) and the use of lavish praise. Further, it makes a lot of dog-sense if our humans, while helping us overcome our fear, also trained us to be well behaved in the car (but that's for the next book!).

Slade, I recognize that I didn't write about some of the reasons you and other canines may be fearful of the car like accidents, eye damage, heat exhaustion, death, etc. Even so, I've found that life is about taking the good with the bad and that you can't have one without the other. And, I've learned not to let my fears, particularly when it's of something remote and unlikely, get in the way of my enjoyment and happiness. Riding in the car is something I enjoy and look forward to, and I hope that one day you will regain the joy of riding you once had. Meanwhile...I've got "shotgun"!

Curtis the Dog

"Did you ever notice when you blow in a dog's face he gets mad at you? But when you take him in a car he sticks his head out the window!" - Steve Bluestone

NOT ALL DOGS LOVE CARS (OR TRUCKS)

It's not unusual for dogs to have behavior problems related to the car such as fear-of-riding, car-sickness, and unruly, hyperactive or territorial behavior that gets them into trouble. Additionally, cars pose a number of significant risks to dogs, including eye damage, being hit by cars, contributing to and being a victim of car accidents, falling out of a car (or back of a pick-up) and heat stroke from being left in a closed car during warm weather.

"Dogs feel very strongly that they should always go with you in the car, in case the need should arise for them to bark violently at nothing right in your ear." - Dave Barry

I THINK I'M GONNA BE SICK!

Should your dog start becoming sick in the car, crack open a window for some fresh air and allow them to see the road ahead as a way of orienting themselves. Sometimes, for dogs with "severe" cases, or when being taken on a relatively long trip, it may make some dog-sense to try some motion sickness medication from the vet.

IT'S THE STRESS NOT THE MOTION

Motion can cause car-sickness in a dog but it's usually stress or anxiety that causes them to yawn, excessively drool and sometimes hurl their kibble. Whining and running around are also signs of impending sickness, which can occur as soon as a dog knows it's in for a car ride.

CONDITIONING THE DOG TO LIKE THE CAR

Start by sitting in the car with the dog. Read, listen to music and DON'T start the engine. Repeat this for several days until the dog seems comfortable. If it gets sick, re-start the process with shorter periods of time. Once the dog is comfortable, not fearful and not sick, start the engine but DON'T go anywhere. Once the dog is fine with that, the next step may be to back out of the driveway and then back in, followed by a short trip, perhaps just around the block. Eventually, take the dog to enjoyable places, like a park, beach or friend's house so they learn to associate car rides with fun, pleasant and rewarding events. Of course, don't rush the process to avoid "one-step-forward-two-steps-back", and the dog should be praised for not being sick and fearful.

"One dog barks at something,
the rest bark at him."
- Chinese Proverb

LAST BARK

I hope that you enjoyed "Ask Curtis" and found my advice to be entertainingly informative and helpful.

Should you or any humans in your life have any issues with which I could help, or an observation on which I could comment, please email me at curtis@askcurtisthedog.com. Recognizing that electronic communication may not be comfortable for some, you can also write me at:

Ask Curtis

29636 Quail Run Drive

Agoura Hills, CA 91301

If you're writing to me the old fashioned way, please be sure to include a return address!

Finally, while I prefer to dispense my dog-sense for dogkind and humans, letters seeking advice or comment from other animals, including cats, are welcome and will be responded to in as respectful a manner as I can muster!

Barkingly yours,

Curtis the Dog

P.S. And, please visit www.askcurtisthedog.com

"Magnetism is one of the Six Fundamental Forces of the Universe, with the other five being Gravity, Duct Tape, Whining, Remote Control, and The Force that Pulls Dogs Toward the Groins of Strangers." - Dave Barry

"In order to really enjoy a dog, one doesn't merely try to train him to be semi-human. The point of it is to open oneself to the possibility of becoming partly a dog." - Edward Hoagland

"All knowledge, the totality of all questions and all answers, is contained in the dog." - Franz Kafka

"I've seen a look in dogs' eyes, a quickly vanishing look of amazed contempt, and I am convinced that basically dogs think humans are nuts."
- John Steinbeck